ivan petrov

ivan petrov
russia through a shot glass
by c. s. walton

garrett county press
1999

All rights reserved. Printed in the United States of America. No part of this book may be used or reproduced in any manner whatsoever without written permission from the publisher except in the case of brief quotations embodied in critical articles and reviews.

For more information address
Garrett County Press, 828 Royal Street. #248, New Orleans, LA 70116
www.gcpress.com

Garrett County Press books are printed on acid-free paper.

Cover and text design by Gail Carter
Cover photography by Rebecca Nolan

LIBRARY OF CONGRESS CATALOG NUMBER
98-075471

ISBN 1-891053-83-3

author's note

This is a true story. I met Ivan Petrov in a city in the West in 1996. Over the course of two years he told me his life story.

prologue

People ask me: "What was it like?" Well I'll tell them what it was like. Where I grew up—a provincial Russian town in the middle years of this century—it made no difference which side of the barbed wire you lived on. Prisoners in camps, collective farmers, factory workers—one man's life was as bleak as another's.

Some people accepted things as they were and tried to carve out careers for themselves as informers or bureaucrats; others sought a way out.

I chose to become a drunk, not an ordinary, drink-up-your-wage-packet drunk, or even a flog-your-house-and-furniture drunk, but a vagabond and a beggar who became intimate with forests, garbage dumps and railway stations all over our great country. I am *Ivan Pyatii-Pyanets Proklatii:* Ivan the Fifth—Damned Drunkard.

And what of it? As a man I once knew who happened to be a cannibal remarked: "You'd have done the same in my place!"

ivan petrov

chapter one

Sirens wailed as gas clouds billowed through the market place. Pressing our scarves to our faces, we ran with the other shoppers towards the gate. Stall holders fled too, deserting bunches of herbs, beetroot and meat bones. "It's plant Number 14 again," a woman behind us grumbled.

I saw a man reach towards a sausage on a stall. Suddenly a butcher's knife glinted and blood spattered across the thief's coat. A fingertip fell in the mud near me. I wanted to pick it up but my mother pulled me away.

Our block of flats was swathed in yellow fog. We ran upstairs, fastened the windows tightly and sat down to wait for the radio dish in the kitchen to give the all-clear. I felt safe behind concrete and glass, but I worried about the families who lived in the wooden barrack huts below us.

"Mum, what about the people in the barracks? Maybe the gas will get through their walls and poison them?"

"They'll be all right."

As the wind changed the fog began to thin. The great stone figure of Stalin emerged through the mist, rooted to his platform in front of our factory's board of honour. One by one the chimneys of our chemical plants reappeared. At last I could see our pyramids—great piles of Caspian sea salt that Volga barges dumped by the town's chlorine plant.

The district where we lived was called Bersol, after our local factory which manufactured potassium chlorate. Its managers and chief engineers lived in our block of flats; shop-floor workers were housed in the wooden barracks.

Half a mile down the road there was a TNT plant where prisoners worked. Every morning I watched them leave their camp by the railway embankment. When dusk fell and the searchlights came on I saw them shuffling home again with bowed heads. Dogs snapped at their heels. I wondered if my father could be among those grey figures.

'You know Ivan's father was a Chekist...[1],' my grandmother had whispered to a neighbour woman. I did not understand her, although I knew that the man who lived with us was not my real father. I dimly remembered another man, a tall figure walking through the front door with a metal basin on his head. I had not seen that man for a long time.

"Mum, where is that other man who used to live here?"

"He's in prison. Forget about him."

"Can I send him my drawing of the Cutty Sark?"

Slowly, my mother put her knife down on the chopping board. "He is not allowed to receive letters," she said, without turning round.

---

[1] The Cheka was the political police force formed just after the revolution in 1917.

My stepfather's belt was studded like a Cossack's. At school they asked questions about the marks on my skin. I did not know what to say. I was afraid that if I told the truth I would be beaten again. The local Party committee summoned my parents for a consultation. After that my stepfather did not beat me so often but instead he kept me indoors for days at a time.

During those endless days I used to sit in our bay window, sadly watching my friends kick a clod of frozen horse-dung around the yard below. They swooped after their ball like a flock of demented birds. Vovka Bolotin kept goal with his crutch. We all envied Vovka. He used his crutch so deftly it was impossible to attack him even from the side.

Nelka Ehrlich, who lived in the flat opposite ours, often came to play with my sister and me. One morning the kitchen radio dish began playing my favourite song: *Sailing the Seven Seas*. Nelka pranced around making faces to distract me. I hit her and grabbed her pigtails. My mother burst in and pulled us apart. She slapped me but not Nelka.

'She'll be sorry, she'll be sorry...'

I ran into the toilet, climbed onto the seat, looped the washing line round my neck, tied it to a hook and jumped. Black circles closed in before my eyes and I felt myself falling. Then I was lying on the floor and Mum was screaming at me again. My neck hurt.

Nelka and I made up. Her family were kind to me and I spent a lot of time in their flat. One day, sometime after the war had begun, we were playing together at her table when the room dissolved around us. Light bulbs swung, glass shattered and the sideboard toppled over onto Nelka's baby brother. The earth roared and shook. I thought I had better go home. As I crossed the landing the floor heaved again. My mother appeared in the doorway with my sister in her arms. She screamed at me to follow and we ran across the street to the factory offices where a throng of people were hurrying down to the basement shelter.

The door was thick like a submarine's and had a round handle. Someone closed it and we sat down to wait. At first we thought it was an air raid but we heard no planes. German bombers had never come this far into Russia. Then we guessed that one of the munitions factories had blown up. We waited in silence, praying that no spark or ball of flame would drop on our plant and wipe us all out.

Nelka sat opposite me, her face deathly white. Suddenly she retched. She bent her head low and vomited onto the floor. As she straightened again I saw a thin white worm dangling from her lips. It swayed slightly. Then her chest and throat convulsed and she spewed the worm onto the floor. I watched it lying in the pool of sick and tried to imagine it curled up inside Nelka's guts. I wanted to ask her if the worm had tickled, but I guessed it wasn't the right moment.

When the *all clear* sounded we climbed up to the street. It was covered in glass and rubble and there was a large piece of concrete stairwell across the entrance to our block. The windows of our flat were gaping black holes spiked with daggers of glass.

We set off for my grandmother's house on the edge of town. There was a hard frost. Behind us the sky was red with the flames of the burning plant. Sounds of the town faded until the stillness was broken only by my mother's heels clip-clopping on the cobbles.

The next day I saw corpses piled in the snow outside the hospital. They were naked and charred like a roasted pig I had once seen at a country wedding. The explosives plant had blown up just as the workers were changing shifts. Scores were killed, maybe hundreds; no one ever counted. I was happy because our school was closed for two weeks. Its windows had been blown out.

People said it was sabotage and that our town simpleton, Bathhouse Losha, was a German spy. Bathhouse Losha had never harmed anyone, but after a few weeks he disappeared and was never seen again.

Chapaevsk lay on a railway line between the Front and the arms factories in the Ural mountains. Trains loaded with broken tanks and weapons stopped at our station. Some of us boys would distract the guards while the others swarmed over the equipment. I undid copper rings from shells and mainsprings from grenades. I knew a neighbour who would give me a couple of roubles for those. We opened the hatches of tanks and dropped down inside, examining dials and levers, taking them apart to try to understand how they worked. When the train jerked and began to move we scrambled out and leaped off, rolling down the embankment on the far side of the station.

The prisoners in the camp by the railway line had been sent to the Front. Uzbek and Kirghiz peasants took their place. At first they too had gone off to fight, but they did not understand enough Russian to obey orders. When one was killed his comrades would gather around the corpse and wail; then they too were cut down by bullets. So instead of fighting they joined the labour army. Changing their kaftans and skull caps for rubber suits and breathing apparatus, they worked on production lines filling shells with mustard gas and Lewisite.

My mother was a medical assistant at a munitions plant. She told me that the Uzbeks were homesick for their mountain pastures and sometimes slipped off their gas masks for a minute or two. They hoped to fall sick enough to be sent home, or at least to earn a couple of weeks' rest in bed. There are many Uzbek graves in our cemetery.

Everyone gripped tightly onto the person in front of them to keep hooligans from breaking through the bread queue. A man hurried out of the shop, clutching a loaf to his chest. Suddenly a small figure ran at the man and sank its teeth into his wrist, making him yell and drop the loaf. The child fell to its knees and devoured the bread right there on the ground. The man kicked him and tried to pull him up but the boy took no notice. People in the queue tutted and grumbled, but no one moved.

"Well, God sees everything, and the poor things are hungry too," said the old lady behind me. There were many homeless kids in our town. They had run away from the Front and the areas under Nazi occupation.

The next morning I saw the boy-thief crawl out from

under Stalin's feet. I grabbed a piece of bread from our kitchen and ran downstairs. Feeling a bit scared, I held out the bread. The boy took it and stuffed it into his shirt. His face was white and he looked straight through me as blind men do. Before he could run off I asked: "My name is Vanya, what's yours?"

"Slavka."

"Why do you live under the board of honour?"

"I ran away from a children's home in Kharkov. They gave us nothing to eat there. My father was killed on the Front; my mother died when our house was bombed. I'm okay here."

"I can get some potatoes from our store. Come with me and we'll roast them on the slag heap by the TNT plant."

"All right."

I skipped school for the next few days to hang around with Slavka. I admired him almost as much as my literary hero, Robinson Crusoe. His senses were much sharper than mine. If he heard a paper rustle 50 metres away he would stiffen like a hunting dog. One day he suggested: "Vanya, let's run away to the Front. Maybe a regiment will adopt us as sons."

I agreed, and crept out of the house one day with a small bundle of clothes and a loaf under my arm. Slavka showed me how to sneak onto trains. Twice we tried to cross the Syzran bridge over the Volga but soldiers discovered us and turned us back. The third time we wriggled into a dog box fixed underneath a carriage. The wind blew cold although it was summer. I wrapped my jacket tightly around me and closed my eyes, picturing the whole map of Russia spread out before us with our locomotive crawling along it like a toy. I thought I would burst with happiness.

After a long time we emerged at a station. We told the soldiers there that we were orphans making our way back to liberated territory. Young and kind lads, they gave us food and sent us on our way. We jumped trains, travelling inside now, telling the same story until we reached Kharkov. The city had just been liberated and lay in ruins. It smelt like the waste pit behind Chapaevsk's meat-processing plant, only far worse. It made me want to throw up. Before we could explore we were picked up by female officers and sent to a children's home in Tambov.

The law of the jungle reigned in that home. Big boys snatched food from the girls and the younger kids. Slavka stuck up for me but I could not stand the hunger and so I confessed. I was sent back home to Chapaevsk. My stepfather beat me so badly I spent several days in bed. But my mother fed me. I felt bad about leaving Slavka.

One day after the war was over a form came, saying a parcel was waiting for me at the post office. Mum took me to the post office and I handed in my form. It was the first parcel I had ever received. At home I untied the heavy package. Inside was a book from Slavka, a *Herbarium* full of pictures of strange southern plants and flowers. He wrote that he was in an orphanage in Moscow. He had won a trip to an elite children's camp in the Crimea. Even Party members' children had to be top students to go there. Slavka wrote that he would never forget me.

We carried our books to school in gas mask containers lined with plywood. After class we waited by the school gate for the girls. As they emerged we hit them with our bags. We wanted to punish those who told tales; the rest we hit as a warning.

Worse than the girls were the Young Pioneer leaders who hung back after class to report wrongdoers to the teacher. We despised them and excluded them from our games. Once, in an act of bravado, my friend Tolik threw his red scarf into the classroom stove. A meeting was called. One after another, Pioneer leaders sprang to their feet and denounced Tolik with spite in their voices. Afterwards I tried to cheer him up: "Never mind Tolik, better be damned than an honest Pioneer!" But he became less bold after that.

The Palace of Pioneers was in the former church of Sergei Radonievsky. The church had once been the most beautiful building in Chapaevsk, with mosaic medallions of saints adorning its facade. It closed after the revolution. During the war it was turned into an armaments store and camouflaged in thick grey plaster. After a few years the plaster began to fall off. First it crumbled away from the mosaics. A nose emerged, then a forehead, then the stern eye of a saint. As news of the miracle spread the town filled with believers. Petticoat radio summoned them from forests, steppes and even the Ural mountains. The police drove them away but they regrouped at a distance from the church.

Our maths teacher, Savva Stepanovich Liga, took us down to the church after school. He walked slowly on crutches for he had lost a leg in the war. We gathered in front of the church while Savva Stepanovich spoke:

"It is a very simple phenomenon, explained by the laws of physics. The brickwork is rough so plaster clings to it; mosaics are smooth and plaster falls off them quite easily."

His voice was loud enough for the faithful to hear, but the old ladies raised their voices so their prayers would drown out the words of the heretic. They wanted to believe their miracle.

Soon afterwards the medallions were chipped away and a huge glass window put in their place. On Saturdays we children were sent to help with the work.

After we had helped to build the Palace of Pioneers we were sent out to the steppe to plant forests. These bands of trees would stretch from Chapaevsk to the Caspian Sea, and would protect crops from dry southern winds. In the town we planted saplings around our school and along the streets. At first we cared for them, but then our energies were diverted into a campaign to collect scrap metal, and the neglected trees withered and died.

"Pale youth with feverish gaze[2]*,"* the teacher recited.

"This is an example of reactionary poetry," she continued, "How could a boy possibly look like that?"

"It's possible," I piped up.

She looked at me in surprise. "How?"

"Perhaps he had TB."

The class giggled.

"Out!" roared the teacher. I ran past her and soon I

---

[2] from 'To the Young Poet,' Valery Bryusov (1873–1924).

was walking in the spring sunshine, happy to think of the others bending over their books.

I ran down to the railway line, climbed the embankment and marched along the tracks, keeping my eyes fixed on them in the hope of finding a place where an American spy had undone the bolts. I would become a hero by running towards an oncoming train waving a red scarf on a stick. But I had nothing red. I wished I had not left my Pioneer scarf at school. A character in a book would have cut his arm with a piece of glass and soaked a handkerchief with his blood. It was a pity handkerchieves were bourgeois-intellectual relics and I blew my nose with my fingers.

A long-distance train charged past, as though it cared nothing for our town and our lives. I looked up at the faces flashing by and thought they must belong to the happiest people in the world. In the wake of the train I searched for empty books of matches. Their town of origin was stamped on the rough cardboard: *Vladivostock, Tomsk, Khabarovsk*. The names made my head swim.

At dusk I made my way over to the wooden barracks. Throwing open the outer doors I yelled: "Hurrah!" and charged down the corridor, raising my hands high and batting at long-johns and brassieres dangling overhead. Outside the door of my friend Victor's room I whistled our pirate signal.

"Who's there, friend or foe?"

"Crusoe."

Victor's parents sat at the table eating rye bread and potatoes. His grandparents snored in their bed above the stove and his baby brother bawled unheeded in the corner. Victor and I wrestled on the floor until his parents screamed at us to stop. Then Victor picked up his accordion and we sang old folk songs and sea shanties. Even the grandfather got up from the stove to join in the chorus. I was so out of tune he laughed: "Eh, Vanya, a bear must have farted in your ears."

At first Victor and the other boys who lived in the barracks made fun of me because my parents were Party members and we had a nanny. But they were not malicious and soon grew tired of teasing me. I felt comfortable with them for they were not ashamed of poverty and had no pretensions.

Some of the barracks' families were so poor the children had only one pair of shoes between them. In bad weather they took it in turns to go to school. I did not want to stand out from the rest so when I left our flat in the morning I would run down to the basement, take off my shoes and hide them behind the hot-water pipes. One day I came home from school to find my shoes had gone: my trick had been discovered. While my stepfather Dobrinin raged my mother asked why I had done it.

"To be like the rest," I said.

"Vanya, there is nothing admirable about poverty. There is no shame in working hard for a better life."

But it was my mother I was ashamed of. She strutted through the town like a film star in high heels and expensive dresses. Local children jeered as she went by with her nose in the air: "There's shit on your shoes, Madame!" They paraded in her wake, holding their noses and wiggling their bottoms until they collapsed into the mud, hooting with laughter and whistling at her disappearing back. My mother pretended not to hear. She despised the barrack dwellers as only someone who came from that same background could.

My step-grandparents lived in a dacha at Studioni Avrag, a settlement further up the Volga. Before the revolution the Dobrinins had been members of the nobility. Now they were 'former people' and received no pension. They survived by growing flowers. Their neighbours said that flowers were useless and that they should grow tomatoes and cucumbers instead. But Granny loved her gladioli and asters. Her fingers were bent and clawed and in the evenings she complained of back-ache. After supper she would put on her nightcap and gown and retire with her French novel. She kept a porcelain chamber-pot under her bed, for nothing would make her visit the earth closet at night.

Grandad was a quiet man but when he spoke it was to the point. He was always busy in his garden. I helped look after his two goats, making sure they did not jump over the wall to nibble the neighbours' apple trees. Sometimes they escaped and then we heard the neighbour woman chasing them, shouting, "Hey, you hooligans, you Americans, get out of here!"

My grandparent's daughter Ira was tall and strong and fearless. One day she rowed Granny and me across the Volga for a picnic. My mother swam after the boat. She was a good swimmer, but to tease me Granny asked: "Aren't you afraid your mother will drown?"

"No," I replied, "for I have Auntie Ira."

My grandparents complained that the dam being built across the Volga would harm our natural environment, that animals would be driven away and fish would disappear from the river. I knew they were wrong. The dam would give electricity to everyone and bring us closer to communism.

Studioni Avrag was a summer resort for professors and doctors. I used to play with their children. Each year, as August drew to a close, we bade each other farewell until the next summer. One year few of my playmates returned. In their place young and beautiful newcomers arrived in shining black *Emka* limousines. They wore well-cut uniforms and laughed loudly. I caught glimpses of them through fences, gracefully playing volleyball in their gardens. The adults spoke about them in whispers.

I was a white raven amongst these people, for I came from godforsaken Chapaevsk and I tended goats. I had to prove myself. I did not play football well but I could dive off the river ferries. When the boats tied up at the dock I climbed the side to the third deck and launched myself into the air like a swallow. One year a boy dived under the ferry's paddle and was killed. After that the sailors kept a strict watch, making it even more exciting to sneak past them. When they caught us they slapped tar all over our bodies. Then we got into trouble at home, for it took days to clean the tar off.

One day I sat watching an old man fish from the quay. He pointed across the Volga. "You see some strange fish in these parts, my lad. Over there is a place called Gavrilova Field. That is where prisoners go to die, full of dysentry and pellagra. They send them from camps all over the country. They are goners by the time they reach Gavrilova Field."

I ran away from the man. For a long time after that I tried not to think about the place across the river.

I hid behind the latrine with a rock in my hand. Auntie Praskovya came waddling through the mud clutching her squares of newsprint. She was a bad-tempered old lady who chased us boys out of her yard because she said we stopped her chickens laying. I heard the creak of wood and then a sigh. Burying my nose in my collar I lifted the trapdoor and hurled my brick into the cess pit. A loud shriek followed the splash. I ran off, glancing back to see Auntie Praskovya pulling up her drawers. "Ivan Petrov, you'll be an alcoholic when you grow up!"

I laughed at her prediction. I did not like alcohol, although I knew it was the joy of adult life. I had seen them get drunk often enough. Most people drank meths or some other vodka substitute because the real thing was expensive and hard to obtain. Besides, you could never tell what had been added to it; everyone knew someone who had died from adulterated vodka.

We called methylated spirits *Blue Danube*. It was sold for lighting primus stoves and was in great demand. It was even drunk at weddings, with fruit syrup added to the women's glasses. My mother usually drank surgical spirit which she stole from her factory, adding burned sugar to improve the flavour. She sneered at the 'arse-washing' water of the barracks' families, which was home brew made from hot water, sugar and yeast. Every room had a tub of this muddy liquid bubbling away under a blanket in the corner.

On birthdays and holidays the adults gave us children glasses of beer. Knowing what was expected of us we staggered about, clutching at walls. They laughed, but I knew the adults also exaggerated their drunkenness. Victor's father once spent a night in the police cells for pissing against a statue of Lenin. "Lucky I was drunk," he said afterwards. "If I had been sober I'd have got ten years."

My parents also drank at home but I tried to keep out of the way when they had company. One day they insisted I clean myself up and stay at home. As our visitors arrived I sat, bored, in a corner listening to the usual fussy exchange of compliments.

"Oh Anna Konstantinova, what a marvellous spread!" cried our lady guest.

Mum smirked: *"Quantum satis!"* She had laid out a meal on her best crockery, which Dobrinin had brought back from Germany after the war, along with three guns, a cutthroat razor and a radio. He was not an important man and had carried away only two suitcases of war trophies, but that was not the impression he gave. He boasted that he had ridden into Berlin on a tank, and hinted that he had had the ear of General Koniyev himself.

At table, Dobrinin dominated the conversation, beginning with his wartime feats before moving on to even more unlikely subjects: "Anton, Anton Pavlovich that is, always said he preferred vodka to philosophy as a hangover cure."

'Chekhov died the year before you were born,' I thought to myself, 'but our guests won't say so. It won't even occur to them that you might not have known him personally. They are too impressed by your aristocratic origins to ever dream of questioning you.'

Our guests presented Dobrinin with a bottle of vodka for the toasts. My step-father went to the dresser and rummaged about, finally laying his hands on the neck of a cut-glass decanter pillaged from some Prussian farmhouse. As he pulled out the vessel there was a gasp and a giggle. I bolted for the door.

An egg lay in the bottom of the decanter, the result of one of my experiments. I had heard that eggs lost their shape when soaked in strong acetic acid. I tried it and it worked. I rolled the softened egg into a sausage and dropped it into the decanter. Then I poured in cold water and the egg returned to its normal shape, but of course I could not retrieve it. I pushed the decanter to the back of the dresser and forgot about it.

I waited until it was very late. When I came in Dobrinin was snoring on the sofa and Mum had gone to bed. In the morning my stepfather awoke and began to recall the outrage of the day before. I ran out of the door before he could hit me.

I went to my grandmother's. Granny Nezhdanova lived with her son Volodya in a wooden house built on a pile of slag beside the sulphur plant. Long ago Granny and her husband had fetched soil from the steppe to spread around the house but gradually the groundwater rose and poisoned all their plants. Only goosefoot grew as tall as my head. The water from their well was yellow and tasted of TNT. Granny and Volodya lived on potatoes, salted cabbage, bread and milk baked in the oven. My mother was ashamed of her family and rarely visited or sent them money. Granny's husband had died when I was a baby. She survived by buying needles and thread from a local policeman and selling them in the market.

Uncle Volodya was home that day and to cheer me up he suggested I come into the city with him. My uncle was only six years older than me. He had started work when he was fifteen, but he studied at night school and won a Stalin scholarship to Kuibyshev polytechnic. Volodya was very cheerful and sharp-witted. I was proud to go out with my tall uncle, even though he always wore ski boots, winter and summer, to work and to dances.

We trotted off to the station, swinging a pail of baked milk between us. The local train lurched in and we boarded without tickets. The carriage was packed with passengers, squeezed onto wooden benches, all smoking rough tobacco or nibbling sunflower seeds. The floor crunched as we walked. At a stop further down the line we jumped off and ran to a carriage that the conductors had already checked.

At each station beggars struggled aboard and made their way through the carriages, telling stories or singing rhymes. Most were war invalids, missing arms or legs; some had been blinded or burnt in tanks. "I returned half-dead from the Front to find a lieutenant's cap on my peg," said a shabby man, holding out his hand. A legless man rolled through on a trolley, rattling a tin.

> *"I saw it all, I took Berlin,*
> *I wiped out thirty Hun,*
> *I filled buckets with blood,*
> *So give me something for a drink!"*

The beggars had escaped from invalid homes where they had rotted with hunger and boredom. They slept in stations and cold entranceways, with nothing to do but drink to forget their grief. The most unfortunate were the 'samovars', who had lost both their arms and legs. Just after the war you saw them, gathered outside markets and stations, begging from their little trolleys. Their appeals to their 'dear brothers and sisters . . . ' echoed the words of Molotov during the German advance. These days there were hardly any samovars, even in the city.

"Volodya, where have all the samovars gone?"

"They rounded them up and put them in special hospitals. I heard that they managed to kill themselves there. They hauled each other up onto windowledges using their teeth. Then they nudged one another through open windows with their heads. The staff were probably looking the other way."

As the train pulled into a suburb of Kuibyshev furious screams and curses came from the platform. A group of homeless women were fighting their way aboard. They stank of drink and sweat; their bloated faces were bruised. Some carried thin babies which they thrust at passengers as they begged. One of them grabbed my arm. "Little son, for the love of God give me something for the baby!"

There was a blackish crust of dried blood where her nose should have been. I turned away, curling up on the seat and hugging my knees. I wished I had had something to give her.

I enjoyed walking around the city with my uncle, meeting up with his friends and laughing at their jokes.

At the end of the day we returned to Chapaevsk with our empty pail. As we walked down the muddy lane that led to her house Granny's voice reached us: "That puffed-up little tart! Her own mother not good enough for her! Well Nyurochka[3], what does your fancy man get up to when you're on night shift? Don't come crying to your old mother then!"

Granny was in the throes of her weekly drinking spree. Her padded jacket was torn and her headscarf had fallen off into the mud.

Two policemen were staggering around in the mud trying to catch her. Nimbly she dodged their grasp. Suddenly she launched herself at the nearest man: "Fuck you! Parasite!"

She pushed the policeman so hard that he staggered backwards and sank up to his knees in a rut. Granny laughed and lay down on her back in the deepest puddle. "Come and get me you old goats!"

Guessing that they would not want to soil their uniforms, she relaxed, closed her eyes and broke into a dirty song. We went towards her but I hung back behind Volodya.

"Come on, Mum, let's go home," said Volodya calmly.

Granny allowed him to pull her up and she humbly followed him to the house. Once indoors Volodya took off her muddy clothes and made up her bed. Soon she was snoring peacefully. Volodya sat down to scrape the mud off her boots. I took my leave.

Although my mother forbade me to visit Granny I often called on her. I would sit on the wooden bench by

[3] Nyurochka: a diminutive of Anna.

her door and wait for her to come back from the market. One day she stopped at the gate, looking at me tenderly with a jug of her famous milk clutched to her breast. "Ah, shit of my shit, when you're a big boy you'll give your old Granny three kopecks for her hair-of-the-dog."

My grandmother was very good natured when sober. She never bothered me about my homework or my performance at school; she was simply sure that I did better than all the rest. When I told her about my quarrels with my stepfather she cursed him and my mother but did not approve of my attempts to run away. She would send me back home at night.

Perhaps it was because of Granny that I liked neither drinking nor drunks when I was little.

The first time I got drunk was at a new year's party at Victor's house. We laid out a feast of bread and herring and prepared ten litres of home brew from sugar I filched from home. Someone brought a bottle of vodka. Victor's parents watched our preparations with amusement. The next day we felt so terrible we did not want to repeat the experiment for a long time.

By the time I was fifteen I had been drunk no more than a dozen times. I did not yet have the taste for alcohol although I would join my friends for a drink. Besides, it was unwise to come home with spirits on my breath because I had an informer sleeping in my room. Marussya was our nanny. A country girl who could barely read or write, she had been born during the famine of 1920 when babies ran the risk of being stolen and butchered by their starving neighbours. But Marussya survived both the famine and collectivisation. When war broke out she escaped her farm by going to work in a munitions plant. There was a shortage of labour so they did not ask for her passport[4]. Marussya poured mustard gas into shells on a conveyor belt. A partition separated the workers, so that an exploding shell would kill only one person. You don't have to be literate to understand the dangers of such a job. Marussya was happy to come to work for my parents. She stayed with us for twenty years and never married. The war left millions of surplus women and Marussya was last in the queue. Smallpox had blinded her in one eye and left her face pitted and scarred. I called her Cyclops.

With peasant cunning Cyclops noticed that I had no one on my side, so she tried to ingratiate herself with my mother by getting me into trouble. One day she went too far and accused me of stealing her purse. My mother told her to be careful.

"My son may be a hooligan but he is not a thief."

A few minutes later Cyclops was feigning surprise at finding her purse under a pile of clothes.

"As I went out in the summer morn to see my lover off to war . . . " she sang one day as she made pies. I was laughing at the idea of that old maid having a lover when the phone rang. Cyclops thundered out of the kitchen shouting "I'm coming!" as though the caller could hear her. It was Uncle Volodya for me.

"Come to the football match this afternoon. Bersol are playing Kuibyshev Metallurgists."

---

[4] Peasants had no passports, so that they were effectively tied to their collective farms.

I met Volodya at the triumphal entrance arch to Chapaevsk's stadium. It had no stands and no fence separating spectators from the pitch. The teams played with as much gusto as we boys did. Everyone threw themselves into the attack and no one bothered about defence. Just before full time a penalty was awarded to the Kuibyshev side. The spectators rushed onto the pitch and stood around the penalty area yelling abuse at the striker. It worked, because the shot was so weak our keeper saved it with ease. The referee tried to clear the pitch but the crowd threatened to turn him into soap and someone punched him.

Volodya and I streamed happily away from the ground with the other men and boys. Some were taking nips from bottles stuffed into their pockets. The autumn air smelled of damp birch leaves and bonfires. Smoke rose from bathhouses by the river where people were making samogon[5].

We ran into Victor who produced a bottle of *Spirol* from his pocket. This was an alcohol-based medication that was rubbed on the head to cure dandruff. You could buy it cheaply at any chemists. Like many local men Victor's father drank *Spirol*. He also knew prison recipes for preparing alcohol from paint-thinner, furniture polish and glue.

Volodya refused the *Spirol* and went home to look after his mother. It was her drinking day. Victor and I tackled the bottle. The oily potion tasted disgusting, making me want to throw up. But at the same time a

---

[5] Samogon was home-distilled spirits.

warm feeling spread through my head and chest. Suddenly I felt invulnerable. "Victor!" I cried, "I know why people drink!" I burst out laughing and thought I would never stop.

Dobrinin watched me like an eagle, waiting for an excuse to explode. My mother and sister ate in heavy silence. When I could bear it no longer I balanced my knife on the salt pot and span the blade. Dobrinin leapt to his feet, banging the table with his fist.

"You see! You see that little bastard?" he turned to my mother, "I feed him, put shoes on his feet . . . get out! Leech!"

I ran out of the house to my friend Gelka Kazin's. I hoped he would have enough for a bottle of *Spirol* or *Blue Danube*, but that day he had other things on his mind.

"Vanya, I have to get away from this damned place. The neighbours say Mum is a prostitute, just because men come here. I am always getting into fights over it."

Gelka had no father. To make ends meet his mother took in sewing. She mended jackets and ran up shirts and trousers so it should not have been surprising that men came to her room. People in the barracks just could not live without gossip.

Gelka's mother was always kind to me. When she came in I told her about my trouble with Dobrinin.

"Of course he is only my stepfather. My real father is working as a secret agent in a capitalist country. He is not allowed to contact us."

I still hoped that he would turn up one day, when the judges in Moscow realised their mistake. Or perhaps Stalin himself would hear of the miscarriage of justice and grant him a pardon.

"Oh they must have shot him years ago," said Gelka casually.

"No!" I made a headlong rush at Gelka, forgetting that he was our school boxing champion. He pushed me back into the corner. His mother leaped up and slapped his face.

"Get out!" she screamed. "Take no notice, Vanya. I am sure your father is doing valuable and patriotic work." She spoke firmly, but she had tears in her eyes.

Gelka and I patched things up and decided to leave town. We would become sailors. Grandfather Dobrinin wrote to the Moscow naval ministry for a prospectus of all the academies in the USSR. We decided the Archangelsk academy would suit us best. It was on the open sea, unlike Baku or Astrakhan and would be cheaper to reach than Vladivostock. Most important, we knew that there would be less competition than for Odessa or Leningrad. A top student in Chapaevsk was not the same as one in Moscow.

My parents told me not to be in a hurry to leave but I was sure they would sigh with relief when I finally walked out of the door.

chapter two

"How well he plays the balalaika!" we shouted as the boy from Tula awoke, shaking his hands in pain. Gelka had slipped lighted strips of paper between his fingers while he slept.

Boys from all over the country had come to the Archangelsk Naval Academy to sit the entrance exams. Our dormitory was as noisy as a stack of nesting gulls. Gelka and I teamed up with three lads from Chelyabinsk to guard each other at night.

After our exams we wandered the wooden streets of Archangelsk, as drowsy as autumn flies, waiting for our results. Although I did well in the exams the academy rejected me. As my father was an Enemy of the People I was tainted by association; the navy did not want me in its ranks.

When term began we had to leave the academy. My friends and I found an abandoned sea hunter moored near a timber yard. We moved in, building bonfires on deck, drinking vodka, baking potatoes and singing pirate songs far into the night. In the daytime we earned money loading wooden planks on the docks. When the police turned up we explained we were waiting for money from home. They left us alone. Gelka's mother wired his return fare and he went back to Chapaevsk. I was determined to avoid that fate, having tasted freedom for the first time in my life since running away to the Front with Slavka.

Snow began to fall and it became too cold to stay on our ship. I crossed the Dvina to Solombala island, which was the real port of Archangelsk, and found a place in a seaman's hostel.

"There are foreign sailors here," said the hostel's Party instructor. "You must be very careful. If anyone from a capitalist country aproaches you, report it immediately. Do not pick up anything you see in the streets. *Agents provocateurs* put chocolates and attractive magazines in bins so that they can take photos of Russians rummaging through rubbish."

'I wonder if our newspaper photos of American scavengers are taken in the same way,' I thought.

Despite the warnings we nodded and grinned at the foreign sailors. Mainly Norwegians, they were simple men like us, interested in drinking and girls.

I came across *The Wave*, a pre-revolution coal ship, in dry dock in Solombala and on an impulse asked the skipper to take me on as ship's boy. I was not yet sixteen but I pleaded my love for hard work and the sea. In the end he agreed. A few days later we set sail down the Dvina, bound for Spitzbergen.

"When will we see the sea?" I kept asking impatiently.

"Your father will reach the gates of hell first, lad," laughed the sailors, "don't be in a hurry."

As we crossed the Arctic Circle my shipmates baptised me in a tub of sea water. The cold took my breath away until I was revived with tumblers of vodka.

The Barents sea was always choppy. Water sprayed up onto the ship and froze. From morning till night I was breaking ice on the deck, the spars and the rigging. The worst task was cleaning up after coal had been loaded. The sailors liked their ship to shine so I had to swill coal dust off the decks and then wash it out of every nook and cranny with the point of a wet cloth. The incessant rain soaked my oilskins and weighed me down as I worked.

"If you don't pull your weight, boy, you'll be off at the next port," said the bosun. Then he turned to the other sailors: "Anyone who makes fun of this lad will get a punch in the face. Understood?"

We sailed to the Spitzbergen port of Barentsburg, where there was a Soviet mining concession. Convicts worked the mines. Barentsburg was foreign territory and therefore off limits to a son of an Enemy of the People. When the other sailors had gone ashore for the evening I stood on deck looking at the stars and the lights from the port. Only the distant bark of a dog or a drunken shout broke the silence. It seemed that somewhere below the horizon a fire was burning, shooting up pink flares into the heavens. Bars of light striped the sky, bending into weird forms. I felt sorry for the prisoners on shore for I knew their camp floodlights would blot out these northern lights.

Archangelsk was already cut off by the frozen White Sea so on our return voyage we unloaded our coal at Murmansk. The port was surrounded by logging camps. "Be vigilant," warned the *Wave's* political instructor before we disembarked. "The camps are full of criminals and Enemies of the People."

"Convicts slip letters between the logs," the bosun whispered to me. "Sometimes one of them cuts off a hand and nails it to a log. They hope that someone abroad will see it and make a fuss."

I had heard these camp stories before; they surprised me as little as night following day.

Our next voyage was to Igarka in Siberia. We sailed via Franz Josef Land, taking supplies to the meteorologists who worked on Rudolf Island, in the far north of the archipelago. The shore was surrounded by ice floes which crashed against each other so violently we were prevented from landing. We unloaded our cargo onto a sheet of ice and the meteorologists came to fetch it on dog sleds. They waved and shouted greetings, happy to see their first visitors for months. I envied them. The Arctic seemed exciting and romantic to me; people had only been living there for the short time I had been on this earth.

At the mouth of the the Yenisei we took a navigator on board to steer us around the river's islands and shallows. We followed the river for a thousand kilometres down to Igarka. Our political instructor again warned us to be vigilant, as prisoners from the Norilsk camps worked in the town. When I went ashore however, I found it hard to tell the difference between convicts and ordinary people. Some men came up and politely asked us to post letters for them so they could avoid the censor. We all agreed. Later I dropped four letters into a box in Archangelsk.

We sailed back up the foggy Yenisei, through the Kara sea, and past the tip of Novaya Zemlya to Nar'ian Mar, where we had to deliver a *Victory* car to the local Party chief. The car drove us all mad. It got in my way when I swept the deck and its tarpaulin cover kept wrenching loose and flapping like a dirty flag. When I tried to fasten it down it resisted me as though it were alive. Everyone was happy to see the last of the vehicle at Nar'ian Mar. It was a mystery where the Party boss would drive, for there were no roads in the region.

The *Wave* left me behind at Archangelsk. It was bound for the British Isles so they could not take me. The night it sailed I went to a bar and got as drunk as a piglet's squeal. I awoke feeling sick but I had to get up and look for another post before the sea froze over. As

I dragged myself out that morning I saw a sign in the hostel foyer: *Radio-operator training college in Riga seeks applicants. Fare paid.* I wrote and they accepted me.

The boys travelling with me to Riga came from villages deep in the countryside. They had never seen a train before and were nervous of the iron horse. I laughed at the quaint way they spoke: "Yesterday we were to a bar going, vodka drinking, with a soldier fighting."

The Riga train amazed us with its clean toilets and polite conductresses. There were not even any cigarette butts on the floor. Beyond the window, however, war had left its traces in a desolate landscape of ruined buildings. We passed countless wrecks of German tanks. People in their grey padded jackets looked like the convicts of Igarka.

We could not afford restaurant car meals so we bought baked potatoes and cucumbers from old ladies on station platforms. Some potatoes were still raw in the centre. The country boys were shocked. It never would have entered their heads to cheat in this way. People from the north were more honest than us, perhaps because they had never had serfdom. In Central Russia people were still afflicted with the slave mentality and would try anything on if they thought they could get away it, even when there was no point.

The outskirts of Riga were scarred with bombed factories; its centre was pitted with burned-out wooden buildings. We were surprised to find our college undamaged by war. It was a six-storey former hotel with *Ano 1905* embossed on its facade.

I quickly settled into the institute and soon felt liked

and respected by my fellows. The college was a friendly place. When a master punished a boy one evening by withholding his dinner the rest of us tipped our dishes of porridge over the tables. Then we picked up our bread and walked out of the dining room. Perhaps not everyone wanted to go along with this protest but they kept quiet in the face of our collective decision.

My best friend was a boy called Victor Rudenko. He came from Kotlas, where his parents had been exiled as kulaks[1]. Victor had picked up criminal jargon and liked to show off by calling out to the other boys: "You over there with rickets!" or "You ugly bastard!"

Rudenko's bravado backfired, for he became known as 'Rickets'.

There were one or two petty dictators amongst the second year boys. Those who did not have the sense to keep out of their sight were constantly sent out for cigarettes or to take messages to girls at the bookbinders' college. I noticed that some lads—most of them insecure boys from collective farms—actually enjoyed this treatment. "For them life without servitude would be like life without cake," Rickets remarked.

Rickets and I made friends with a Rigan, Valerka Polenov. Valerka was small and his shoulders were raised as though shrugging in bewilderment. He dressed carelessly with his cap pulled down over one ear. His hero was Lord Byron. Half the time Valerka was in a different world. He was not even aware that people respected him. I never found out how he had ended up

---

[1] Kulaks were wealthy peasants who were shot or exiled to Siberia during the collectivisation period of the early 1930s.

in our college; he probably only came because it was next door to his house.

Valerka's father was an administrator at the circus. In his spare time he made records from x-ray films, engraving them with the songs of Vertinsky and Vadim Kozin. If you held a disc up to the light you saw a broken bone or vertebra. I often dropped in on Valerka's father to borrow some of these records, but after those visits I knew I would never again enjoy the circus. To reach the offices we had to walk through the dwarves' quarters. Seeing them up close, I no longer understood why we laughed at them. Without make-up, in the middle of their family quarrels, swearing, drinking and fighting, the dwarves were just like the people in our barracks at home. They were no different to anyone else; you might as well look in the mirror and laugh.

Although I enjoyed college, the place where I really felt I belonged—for the first time in my life—was the town's yacht club. When I saw a notice in the papers appealing for new members I took a tram out to Lake Kish and presented myself. They put me to work scraping paint and collecting rubbish. I threw myself into my tasks, hoping that my dedication to the job would prove my love for the sea. Everyone was busy preparing for the summer, cleaning and painting their yachts which looked like fragile, pretty toys. The friendship of the club was different to that of the institute; you did not have to use your fists to win respect.

When he found out about my visits to the yacht club our college director phoned to tell them I was skipping lessons. He must have known I was jumping the tram to get there and back and so he wanted to stop me going. The club told me they were sorry to lose me and that I should come back in a year's time.

At first I was furious, but there was nothing I could do or I would have been expelled from the institute. After that I filled up my spare time by going out drinking with Rickets. The institute's political instructor had warned us that the town was full of bourgeois elements and the older boys said that the Latvian Forest Brotherhood had been known to catch lone Russians and strangle them. Despite these warnings, Rickets and I took every opportunity to slope off together through the dark streets. A stroke of luck had secured us an evening job unloading potatoes from railway wagons, so we had cash to spend. We usually went to the *Reindeer Antlers*, a back-street joint popular with soldiers and sailors. Patrols did not think to look there. Walking down the steps and throwing open the door of the little basement bar was like crossing into another world, one of warmth and comradeship.

Mixing a cocktail of vodka, beer, salt, pepper, mustard and vinegar I would cry "Down the hatch!" and empty the glass in one. I had learned to do this back in Chapaevsk after watching my friends' parents draining glasses of spirit. I practised with water until I had mastered the technique.

Regular fights broke out in the *Reindeer Antlers*, but were usually stopped before serious injury occured. Not to be outdone, Rickets and I got into a fight with each other at least once a month. It was a ritual between us and meant nothing. Other customers tried to pull us apart but the harder they tried the more tightly we grappled with each other. Finally we would stagger back up the basement steps and roll home with our arms about each other, roaring pirate songs into the damp night air.

The rich kids of Riga called themselves *stilyagi*. They listened to jazz and danced the boogie-woogie. They wore tight trousers and jackets with shoulder-pads as wide as the Pacific Ocean. I liked western music too but I thought those *stilyagi* were spoilt brats. You had to have a father in Party headquarters or a mother in a department store to dress as they did. The Komsomol paper denounced the *stilyagi* as 'spittle on the mirror of our socialist reality'; we just beat them up whenever we could. They were pampered kids and useless at fighting.

That summer we were sent out from the college to work on the *Beria* collective farm. I had never seen such dereliction and misery. The mud was even worse than at home. There was no mechanical farm equipment; only worn-out horses. Our overseer spent his days drinking with the farm chairman. We slept on straw in a shed and were fed on potatoes and rye bread which was half raw and full of chaff. Everyone on the farm ate this food. We skived off to help old people and single women with their private plots in return for food and home brew. The only consolation of farm life was samogon. Everyone distilled it so no one denounced their neighbour. Besides, the local policeman was a villager too.

I could not understand why people lived on that hopeless farm, why they did not run off wherever the wind blew. I was relieved when our forced labour ended and we went back to college. I did not even miss the constant supply of alcohol.

Did you cry when Stalin died? Does the world seem different now? wrote Olga, one of my former classmates in Chapaevsk, in a letter to me that March. Stalin's death unsettled us all. For some reason everyone started to speak in whispers, as though his corpse were lying in the next room. I took my place in the guard of honour by his portrait. We assembled in the sports hall to listen to the funeral broadcast. Some boys cried. I felt sad too and strangely insecure. Then Rickets started a game of push and shove in the back row and I cheered up.

We were being prepared for work in remote Siberian stations where there would be no phone connections. We would have to know how to repair our equipment when it broke down. The more they told us about the difficulties that lay ahead the prouder we felt of our profession. We looked down on boys from other colleges; weren't there already millions of fitters and lathe operators in this world?

Everything seemed to be going well for once in my life. Then in my final spring at the college there was a room search and a banned book was found among my things. The book was nothing special, just a dry work on atavistic memory lent to me by Valerka's mother who was a librarian at the Academy of Sciences. Nevertheless, I was summoned to the director's office.

"Where did you get this book?" the director banged his fist on the desk. "Who gave it to you? I demand you tell me! Do you want to be expelled?"

I wondered what to do. I was honour-bound to return the book to Valerka. On an impulse I suddenly snatched it from the director's hand. He halted in mid-sentence as I ran out of the room.

I gave Valerka back his book. It would have looked bad for the college if I had been expelled for reading banned literature so I escaped with a reprimand.

The following Saturday I was chatting to some girls from the bookbinder's college when our new teaching assistant came up. "Got any more subversive literature?" he asked me. Turning to the girls he said: "Our Ivan here really caused a scandal last week."

"It's none of your business!" I shouted.

He just laughed.

"Okay you bastard," I cried, swinging a punch at him. I had already had a few beers and did not stop to consider that the assistant was twice my size. He knocked me to the ground as easily as if I had been a flea.

"Take him away, lads," he said to some of my classmates who had gathered to watch the fight. They picked me up and carried me off to my room. Rickets and I had hidden a bottle of vodka in his locker. I started the bottle by myself. The more I drank the worse I felt. Rickets still did not return and before I knew it I had finished the bottle. Some boys appeared at the door and began to tease me. I flung the empty bottle at them, then climbed onto the window ledge and jumped.

The ground seemed to rear up and hit me with shocking force. I lay face down on the cobbles, stunned by pain. 'I'll keep still for a couple of minutes. It will give the others a fright,' I thought. The smell of vomit filled my nostrils. Twisting my neck slightly, I saw one of my classmates throwing up in the gutter. 'Why's he doing that? Can't he hold his drink?' I wondered.

"Don't move, Vanya, we've called an ambulance," said another boy in a shaky voice.

As I was heaved onto a stretcher I caught sight of the scared face of the assistant.

"Excuse me for causing all this trouble," I managed to grind out the words with heavy sarcasm.

The ambulance drive to the hospital seemed endless. Thirst seared my mouth all night. I screamed and swore until I lost consciousness on the x-ray table.

I awoke in agony and confusion. Both my legs and my right arm were covered in plaster. I had a vague impression that my mother had been near me.

"Well, young man," said the doctor, "You have eighteen fractures and your right kidney is damaged. It seems you broke your fall on some telegraph wires and that saved your life. Your mother was here. She stayed until we knew you were out of danger."

I did not want to live. They gave me four shots of morphine a day but it scarcely helped. I pleaded with a God I did not believe in to grant me a break from the relentless pain for just five minutes. I could not face the endless hours ahead, knowing there would be no respite until nightfall when the nurse brought my sleeping tablets. With a great effort of will I managed to save some of these tablets and stored them until I had 14. Then I swallowed them all at once. They resuscitated me and pumped my stomach. After that a nurse watched as I took my medicine.

I stopped eating so they roused my appetite with wine bought with money the college had sent in for my food. When the money ran out they gave me diluted surgical spirit.

My arm and left leg began to heal and they removed the cast but the pain in my right leg increased until it was pulsating in violent waves throughout my body. I pleaded with the doctors to take the plaster off. They ignored me: "It's just the cast squeezing," they said. When they finally removed it they discovered that festering matter had eaten away the cartilege around my knee.

My doctor, Professor Jaegermann, would not listen to my pleas to amputate my leg. He kept draining the knee which had swollen to the size of a football. You could circle my upper thigh with your fingers.

I liked morphine. It seemed to wrap my pain in cotton wool and hold it at a distance, at least for a while. I asked for shots both before and after my dressings were changed but after a while they said I was taking too much and refused to give me any more. My pleas fell on deaf ears. Finally an old French ward sister told me that some of my shots had been nothing more than saline solution. I sent them all to hell and sulked, but I reasoned that if I had managed without morphine before I could in the future.

Gradually my spirits brightened as I began to mix with the other patients. "Let's see the champion of jumping without a parachute," the TB sufferers said, as they clustered round my bed to breathe in the smoke from my cigarettes. The men cracked jokes and shared cakes and vodka that their wives had sent in.

I began to sit up and do exercises. Professor Jaegermann told me I would never be able to bend my leg again but I would eventually be able to walk without crutches.

A few months later I was sent out beyond Vladivostock to Primorskii Krai. I wanted to bury myself in the taiga[2] far away from human eyes. My friends had already left for their Siberian posts. Valerka went to Yakutia. I heard that Rickets had fallen under a tram in Omsk. His injuries were worse then mine and he was sent back to his parents. I never heard from him again.

The Moscow-Vladivostock express was packed with labour recruits[3] desperate to make their pile of gold in the East. Some had spent years in prison camps; others were escaping collective farms. Old hands bragged about the fortunes they had made in logging or mining and the adventures they had had drinking up their pay.

By the time we reached Kazan we were on first name terms and sharing our food. Like every carriage on every long distance train in the country, ours had its joker, its card trickster, its story teller, and its drinkers. We were even blessed with a pair of newlyweds. The husband Mitya was an unpleasant young Komsomol activist: so possessive of his wife that he prevented her from alighting at stops to stretch her legs. His bride Lena did not seem suited to him at all and we wondered what could have brought about their union.

It turned out that Mitya and Lena had been at medical school together in Voroshilovgrad. When they graduated they were posted to Sakhalin. Lena had never been away from home before and she was afraid to travel such a long way by herself, so she took Mitya as

---

[2] The taiga is an area of marshy pine forest that covers most of Siberia.
[3] Labor recruits were offered bonuses to work in Siberia for a minimum of one year.

her husband and protector.

A young sailor in our carriage took a fancy to Lena. He confided in me as we stood smoking in the little space between carriages: "Ivan, do me a favour and set up a game of chess with Mitya. I want to have a word with his wife."

The sailor lured Lena into the smoking compartment where he dripped words of honey and poison into her ear. They seemed to work, for the clandestine affair continued through western Siberia and along the Amur. I doubt whether Lena even noticed Lake Baikal or the bust of Stalin carved into a mountain near Amazar. The rest of us did our best to keep the unsuspecting Mitya occupied.

Finally Lena made up her mind. At Khabarovsk she hid in the next carriage with her sailor while Mitya alighted alone. He wept as he sorted out his belongings. I almost felt sorry for him. Still, he would surely forget Lena as he forged his Party career.

I said goodbye to Lena and her sailor when we reached Vladivostock. As I watched them walk away through the station I wondered if the sailor would live up to his promises. Then I put on my rucksack and caught a tram to the Central Meteorological Office, headquarters for the entire Far East region.

HQ gave me news of my friend Valerka Polenov. He had reached his station in Yakutia to find that all the staff there had been murdered. The crime had been committed by a local Yakut in a drunken rage. Valerka arrived to find the murderer waiting for him in a calm and sober state. Together they buried the murdered men and then the Yakut waited while Valerka radioed for help. I never heard what became of my friend after that, but I doubted that life could have held many more terrors for him.

I was sent to work as second radio operator aboard the *Franz Mehring*. We sailed to weather stations around the Sea of Okhotsk, bringing food, kerosene and alcohol. This spirit was 95 degrees proof, for normal vodka freezes in Siberian cold. Drunk neat or mixed with a handful of snow, it was the hardest currency in the region. A bottle got you anything you wanted. The meteorologists greeted us as though we were long-lost relatives and together we toasted our arrival.

On its return voyage the *Franz Mehring* put me ashore at Adimi point. I was to go inland to work as a radio operator at the village of Akza. An Udegey[4] called Viktor Kaza joined me, with a couple of meteorologists who were travelling even further into the taiga. We put our belongings on a horse and cart and set off on foot. I had never dreamed it would be so hard to walk on crutches. Towards the end of the day I became exhausted and threw away my heavy coat. Viktor noticed and went back to fetch it for me.

Our first stopping place, Samarga, was a miserable collection of moss-covered wooden huts strung out across an isthmus within a bend of the river. There was a fishing collective, an elementary school and a hospital. The buildings were raised on stone piles to protect them from flooding. Long tables for gutting fish stood outside.

---

[4] The Udegey are a Siberian people who live on the eastern seaboard of the Primorye region. Today they number about 1,400. They were nomadic hunters until forcibly settled in the 1930s.

The debris was eaten by gulls or washed away by storms. The air stunk of rotten fish. I used to think the cries of sea birds romantic, but in Samarga they reminded me of the drunken beggar-women on Chapaevsk trains.

The Samarga was a fast-flowing mountain river which took great skill to navigate. Victor Kaza arranged for a fellow Udegey, Shurka Grouse-Catcher, to guide us upriver. However Shurka was busy drinking up his pay from a previous journey and a week passed before he was sober enough to steer a boat again. Eventually we set out in an ulmaga, a long boat made from a hollowed tree trunk. Its prow was flattened into a shovel shape so that it would glide over submerged rocks. At waterfalls we climbed out and walked upriver while Shurka and his son carried the boat on their shoulders.

Shurka Grouse Catcher punted the boat from the prow while his wife paddled from the stern. Their son lay on the floor of the boat sucking lump sugar. I feared that at any instant the ulmaga would overturn or be split by a rock. Shurka deployed great skill in keeping it head on into the current; if he had misjudged an angle the boat would have swung around and been swept off downstream.

Back in Samarga I had watched Shurka sign his contract with us. The sweat had stood out on his forehead as he struggled to steer a pencil across the paper. Yet with a boat pole in his hand he was a virtuoso, reading the river like a book. Unbothered by midges, he took advantage of every break to catch fish or shoot a grouse.

Later, when we reached our destination Shurka came to me in a temper because he had had some money deducted from his pay 'as a tax on childlessness'.

"I have eleven children," he said.

"You have to fill in a form," I explained.

He looked at me in astonishment.

"Don't worry, I'll fill in your forms for you. Here, let's toast Dalstroi[5]."

I opened a bottle of vodka and Shurka calmed down.

Akza was a cluster of 20 huts, an elementary school, a shop and a medical post. The clubhouse had burned down the year before. A few dozen Udegey and nine Russians lived in the village. A man from Leningrad named Kryuchkov had been there since 1924. After graduating from university he had contracted TB. The doctors advised him to leave Leningrad's damp and foggy atmosphere. Every Udegey family in Akza had a child who resembled Kryuchkov.

Dr. Yablonsky was also from Leningrad. Once he had been head of a university department and had known four languages, but he was exiled during the purge of the Leningrad intelligentsia[6]. Now Yablonsky had the shaking hands and watery eyes of an alcoholic. He had forgotten his European languages long ago and learned Udegey in their place.

A third Russian was Pasha Dyachkovsky, a skilled hunter with luxuriant curving moustaches. He was married to a local Udegey woman, Duzga. When drunk Pasha wet his bed and then he would beat his wife mercilessly.

A few days after my arrival we gathered for a drink to celebrate Pasha's birthday. After a while he felt the urge to urinate. He rose from the table, grabbed Duzga

---

[5] Dalstroi was the collective name of the northern Siberian camps.
[6] This purge began after the murder of Kirov in 1934.

and started pulling out her hair in clumps as though they were carrots. We leaped up to restrain him but this offended his soul to the core. He went home, barricaded himself in, climbed up to the attic with his gun and took aim at anyone who came within his field of vision. This was serious, as he lived above the shop which Duzga ran. We needed to buy food. Fortunately Pasha decided to go hunting in the taiga the next day.

"He usually conquers his hangover this way," Dr Yablonsky explained.

There was very little to do in Akza apart from hunt and drink. I could not hunt because of my leg, so I made myself popular by filling in for the observers when they were out hunting or too drunk to work. Of course I drank too, but I had a good stomach for vodka. Even after two bottles I could tap out: 'The weather report from Akza is . . . '

I thought myself Jack-the-Lad because I had studied in Riga, which was almost Europe. I must have got on everyone's nerves, swaggering about, spitting out words between my teeth and calling the women 'darling'. One evening when we were gathered for a drink I grew very excited. Leaping onto a chair I started to declaim some of Yesenin's poems.

"Do any of you understand these lines? Buried out here in the taiga you have never known the world he describes—or you've already forgotten it."

The next day it occured to me that Kryuchkov had seen Yesenin in the flesh. I realised I should apologise to him, but somehow I could never bring myself to do so. I kept out of Kryuchkov's way after that, hanging back if I saw him enter the shop ahead of me.

In my spare time I liked to pack a bottle, a book and some food in my rucksack and walk into the taiga. Then I would stop beneath a tree, open my bottle and settle down to read. Usually however, my attention wandered and I became absorbed by my surroundings. The taiga was lovely. I had never imagined that this earth could be so beautiful. I was surrounded by hills clothed in larch and cedar. Where there had been a fire and the trees had not yet grown back the slopes were covered in brilliant red flowers. I had no regrets then that I had left 'civilisation'.

The other Russians did not share my enthusiasm. When I praised the beauty of the taiga to Pasha, he snapped, "Go and play in the dirt you young wipe-snot," and strode off.

For the first time in my life I had my own room. It contained a stove and a camp bed. A door from the burned-down club served as a table with blocks of wood for stools. The pile of deerskins I slept on was as soft as a feather bed. One day I happened to mention to Victor Kaza that I was looking for cooking utensils. "Come with me," he said, and led me out into the taiga. In a small clearing we came upon a larch which had been festooned like a Christmas tree with aluminium spoons, pans and pieces of cloth.

"In my grandfather's time we laid the dead person in an ulmaga and hung it from the tree," said Victor. "We put berries and salted mushrooms in the boat. The dead had everything they needed for their journey into the next world."

Victor untied a frying pan and gave it to me. I felt a little sorry for him as he was a misfit among the other

Udegey. His hunched back prevented him from hunting and he tried to compensate for this by flaunting his seven years' schooling. This was useless as the Udegey regard hunting far more highly than literacy. Victor had a mentally-retarded Russian wife. I do not know how she ended up at Akza but it was obvious she had been in a labour camp.

"Lyuba you haven't put your knickers on," Pasha cried out one day as she passed by.

Lyuba grinned and lifted the hem of her skirt over her head to reveal bright crimson bloomers. We all laughed at her until Victor emerged from their hut.

"Lyuba, pull your *chemise* down," he scolded, as he pulled her indoors. The watching Udegey roared with laughter again, this time at Victor's pretension.

When February came round the entire settlement gave itself up to an orgy of drunkenness. The occasion was the pelt collector's annual visit. This man was Tsar, God and high court judge rolled into one. He rode up the frozen Samarga to buy furs, accompanied by horse sleighs laden with goods for Duzga's shop.

The pelt collector brought enough cash to pay three or four hunters. This was the only time of the year that the Udegey saw money, although they sometimes earned a little by guiding geologists or doing some building work. They went to the pelt-collector one by one. The first to approach him were his relatives and drinking partners. No one dared cross him or he would refuse to buy their 'soft gold', which was a state monopoly. After a day or two the collector went to Duzga and took back the money that the hunters had spent in her shop. With this cash he paid the next group. This process lasted till all the hunters' pay was in Duzga's pocket and from there, of course, it went back to the state.

The Udegey drank for days on end, silencing their babies with rags soaked in vodka. A few women had the foresight to take cash from their husbands' pockets to buy flour, sugar, salt and dress material. The rest had to spend the year humbling themselves before Duzga, who gave credit because she enjoyed having people in her debt. She was the most powerful person in Akza and you had to take care not to make an enemy of her. When they had drunk all their pay the Udegey went to sleep. A few days later the men emerged with their guns and headed out into the taiga again.

One day an old Udegey known as Grandad Chili dropped in on me unannounced. I bustled about trying to make him comfortable, brushing cigarette butts and paper off a stool. He sat smoking roll-ups in silence. After half an hour he rose and walked out without a word. I was worried, thinking that I might have done something to offend him. I did not want to cross Grandad Chili for I knew he had once killed a Russian teacher out of jealousy. When the police came for him he had gone out and hidden in the taiga for a long time. No one in the village denounced him.

I told Dr Yablonsky about the old man's behaviour. "Don't worry," he reassured me, "The Udegey only speak when they want to sell you something or buy vodka. That was simply what they call 'paying a visit'. He must like you. If you ask him he'll show you his piece of quartz that has a seam of gold in it as thick as a finger. Last year he showed it to some geologists who were passing through here. He said he knew a place where there were many more like it. They hired him as a guide in return for as many cans of condensed milk as he could drink. He led them by the nose for a few weeks until finally he confessed he had forgotten the place. They went back to the coast and now he is waiting for more prospectors this summer. The Udegey know what will happen if geologists find gold in the region."

After that I felt more comfortable with the taciturn Udegey. 'We are supposed to be civilised,' I thought, 'yet we waste so much effort on words which are usually meaningless and often cruel and deceptive.'

In summer the clubhouse was finally repaired and to mark the occasion Samarga sent up the film *The Age of Love* with Lolita Torres. For once the Udegey showed excitement, even bringing babes in arms and their beloved dogs to see the film. The projectionist was drunk and mixed up the reels but no one noticed.

I had hoped to save some money during my posting in the East but it proved impossible. As soon as I received my pay I went over to Duzga to stock up on vodka. I decided to move to Yuge, the most remote station in the Primorye region. There was nowhere to spend money in Yuge so my wages would be saved for me in Samarga.

I set off for Yuge with a convoy of sledges bringing the annual delivery of post and supplies. There was a severe frost so we all had a good drink before we left and topped up along the way. As I could not walk over the rugged terrain I was strapped onto a sledge. While it was mounting an incline my horse stumbled and fell, dragging my sledge after it. The horse broke its leg and had to be shot. The sledge rolled on top of me, leaving me grazed but otherwise unhurt, or so I thought. They gave me vodka and tied me to another sledge. By the time we reached that night's resting place I had sobered up enough to realise that I had broken my leg. In the morning I was sent back to hospital in Samarga.

The hospital had neither electricity nor plaster of Paris. It was staffed by a doctor, a nurse and a medical assistant called Ivan Ivanich, who drank continually out of home-sickness. In the morning Ivan Ivanich's hands shook uncontrollably and I had to light his cigarettes. The doctor despised him so much that she refused to let him help reset my leg. While the nurse shoved a phial of ether under my nose the doctor pressed on my leg with all her strength. After a sharp pain I came to and saw both women lying unconscious on the floor. The inexperienced nurse had released too much ether. My leg had to be put in splints again. It grew back curved like a sabre from hip to ankle.

My deformity made me horribly self-conscious. I had been thinking it was time I got married but now my hopes failed. 'What woman would want to marry a man with a leg like mine?' I wondered. 'I don't want to end up with a wife like Victor's Lyuba.'

HQ offered to send me to the coast but after all I had suffered I wanted to be as far from civilisation as possible. I insisted on going to Yuge, so they sent me up on another sledge and I began work there.

In Yuge I learned that insects are truly the scourge of the taiga. Our observation station was full of bugs and the grass outside crawled with encephalitis ticks. Every time I crossed the threshold of my hut I had to strip off and examine myself from head to foot. Down by the river where there was little wind the midges surrounded me in clouds, biting straight through gauze into my skin. They made mosquitoes seem as harmless as butterflies. The only way to live in the taiga was to be like Shurka Grouse-Catcher and take no notice of midge-bites.

Winter came as a relief, but by then my tobacco had run out and I nearly went insane. Thoughts of cigarettes filled my days and my dreams at night. I pulled out all the butts that had fallen between floorboards. One morning I remembered a place near the river where I had tossed a half-smoked cigarette three weeks before. When daylight came I went out and filled a bucket with snow from that spot. I melted the snow on the stove and struck lucky, fishing out the soggy butt, drying and smoking it. I had never enjoyed a smoke so much in my life, but within ten minutes I was prising up floor boards again.

I grew bored with life in the deep taiga. Work took up no more than two or three hours a day and there was nothing to do for the rest of the time. There were no books. I even missed the society of Akza. Yablonsky had been rehabilitated and returned to Leningrad. I never did apologise to Kryuchkov; it was somehow difficult to do so. He died in the spring as TB sufferers often do.

I started to think more and more about my penfriend Olga Vorobyova in Chapaevsk. We had corresponded since my college days. Olga was a pretty, down-to-earth girl. Most importantly, I had written to her about my leg and it did not seem to bother her. Her letters were full of questions about my plans for the future. I began to think about returning to a normal life. 'Perhaps I'll ask Olga to marry me,' I thought, 'With the money I've saved here I could rent a room from someone so we won't have to live with our parents.'

I was relieved when my three-year posting came to an end and I was able to leave for Vladivostock. On the way I collected 120,000 roubles in Samarga. That was a fabulous sum. Back at home it would take a factory worker several years to earn that amount. I stayed in Samarga for two weeks waiting for the sea-route to open. The shop had run out of vodka but there was a good supply of champagne. When he went home for dinner the shopkeeper locked Ivan Ivanich and me in the shop and we continued to work through the bottles. In the evening we counted the empties and I paid. There was no other way to pass the time. The local women did not appeal to me: after years of gutting fish their buttocks sagged so low they had to lift them up with their hands when they went to sit down.

In the morning before the shop opened I liked to chat to the shopkeeper's paralysed son. He listened open-mouthed to my tales of Riga and Moscow.

"But why do they build the houses so tall?" he kept repeating. "Why do people want to live on top of each other?"

I can't remember much about my return to Vladivostock, except that the first thing I did was go to a barber's. My hair had not been cut for three years and local kids followed me around, jeering at me as though I was some sort of hermaphrodite. After I had cleaned up I went to a restaurant and was soon sending bottles to every table. I was overjoyed to be back in civilisation again and spent a riotous month celebrating the event. At least I had the foresight to buy my ticket home before I blew all my wages. I arrived back in Chapaevsk with a blinding hangover and 68 roubles in my pocket.

chapter three

"Goosie, goosie, goosie!"
 "Hee, hee, hee!"
 "Ten by three?"
 "Me, me, me!"

My workmates and I emerged from the shower room in troikas[1]. One man in each group ran off for a bottle while the other two went to order some snacks.

In the canteen we were held up by a woman from the shop floor who was already drunk and arguing with the server: "I asked for soup—what are these slops?"

"Okay Zhenya, move on, we want to get finished tonight," said the serving woman.

"What do you know about work? We're up to our knees in DDT all day."

"If you don't like the job go somewhere else."

"Someone has to do it."

"Get a move on ladies," shouted my drinking-partner, Lyokha-Tuba.

---

[1] It was customary for a troika of three men to pool ten roubles to buy a bottle of vodka.

Zhenya rounded on him: "And what do you men know about hard work? You technicians sit around on your arses all day while we're getting ourselves in a sweat."

"With Igor Fyodorovich in your case," remarked the serving woman.

Everyone started screaming then, so Lyokha and I gave up on bread and pickles and sat down to wait for our mate. He came running in with the bottle, sat down and poured out three glassfuls. I raised mine: "To women."

"The trouble with this place," Lyokha remarked, "is that however long you spend in the shower you still come out smelling of DDT."

"Yeah, it makes me feel as though I'm crawling with lice[2]," I said. "Never mind. The whole town envies us for breathing in this crap all day long, but what's the use of getting the higher pensions they promise if we don't live long enough to enjoy them?"

"It could be worse. How many of those poor sods who made mustard gas before this place was converted are still alive?[3]"

"My mother does okay," I observed. "For a dose of Lewisite she trots off to a sanatorium in the Crimea each year."

"Funny how Party lungs are more sensitive than anyone else's," said Lyokha.

Lyokha's face and hands were a bright tomato-red

---

[2] DDT was used to get rid of lice.
[3] After the war plants that had made chemical weapons were converted to pesticide production.

colour, making him look like an even heavier drinker than he already was. A couple of weeks ago a woman worker had sprinkled potassium manganese on his head while he slept. When he stood in the shower after work the powder dyed him a deep red. It was taking a long time to wash out and everyone laughed at him, especially the women.

That woman had been getting her revenge on Lyokha for a trick he had played on her. It was the custom of night-shift workers to take forty winks behind their gas masks. One night Lyokha crept up as she slept and painted black ink over the goggles of her mask. Then he shook her awake, shouting: "Fire!". She awoke in terror and blindly leaped into the water tank. Unfortunately it was empty and she broke her arm. She could not complain because she should not have been sleeping and besides, no one grassed on their fellow workers.

After we had drunk the bottle I put on my beret, slung my gas-mask container over my shoulder and said goodbye to my friends. I had a date with my former classmate and penfriend Olga Vorobyova.

Now that I was back in Chapaevsk Olga and I were talking of getting married. The problem was finding somewhere to live. The waiting list for a flat was twenty years. In the meantime I could not live with my parents and I would not live with hers.

Olga worked as a gynaecologist in a local clinic. That night she took me out on her rounds in the ambulance, disguising me in a white coat. It was interesting to see the inside of other people's houses, although they all looked alike. At midnight I struck lucky, for while Olga was attending an emergency I managed to pinch some morphine from her supply and inject myself. I had not lost my taste for the drug.

The first months of our marriage were happy ones. We moved into a flat of our own in Stavropol-on-the-Volga, where communism had almost been built[4]. The Kuibyshev HEP project had flooded old Stavropol and convict labour was building a new town on the banks of the reservoir. I went over and found a job in a synthetic rubber factory. After three months the plant allocated me a flat and Olga came to join me.

We lived like everyone else, going with the flow like shit down the Yenisei. Our one-room flat had a toilet and running water. Olga's parents gave us a table and a bed. After a year my factory presented us with a ticket in the waiting list for a washing machine.

Of course I drank a bit, especially on payday which my workmates and I celebrated wherever we could. We usually went to the barracks where there were several single women who were eager for company. As the night wore on one or two of the lads might wander off home but few could bear to leave their battle stations. Although none of us was an enthusiast for front-rank Soviet labour, our conversation centred around work—there was nothing else to talk about.

Sometimes a wife would turn up at the door, shouting and spoiling our party. Olga never humiliated herself this way, but she would occasionally send one of

---

[4] The Kuibyshev dam and hydro-electric power plant, built by prison labour, was completed in the early 1960s and hailed by the government as 'the building of communism.'

my more restrained friends to fetch me home.

My friend Lyokha followed me to Stavropol. He found a job at my plant and he and his wife moved into a flat in our building. One Sunday I had come home to find a crowd gathered in our courtyard. I pushed my way through and saw Lyokha standing on his balcony, wearing only his vest and long johns. A horse stood placidly beside him. I recognised it as the sad old mare that pulled the beetroot cart to the grocery store below. Wild-eyed and dishevelled, Lyokha was calling raucously to his wife: "Masha, Masha, come here sweetie! I want to introduce you to this fine stallion. Perhaps he can satisfy you, my dear? You might refuse me but not him, surely?"

Lyokha's wife emerged from the building and took off down the road like a startled hare. The crowd swelled, shouting their encouragement as Lyokha delivered a drunken speech about his wife's coldness. The police arrived. The horse refused to budge so the fire brigade had to be called to winch it down.

Lyokha was sent to prison camp and his wife moved in with a local policeman.

It took a lot of vodka to make me drunk, so no one noticed at work if I was slightly intoxicated. I started the day with a hair-of-the-dog, had a top-up at lunchtime and began to drink in earnest in the evening. Vodka was my reward for a dangerous and boring job.

When the government passed a decree against drinking in factory canteens we produced our own spirit on the shop floor. This syntec, as we called it, was made by pumping air through buckets of triethylphosphate. The acidity of the carbon dioxide in the air separated ethyl alcohol from the phosphoric acid. Holding our noses and closing our eyes against the fumes we knocked back our syntec in the showers, leaving before the full effect hit us.

One December a law was passed against public drunkenness. A boss, neighbour or relative could ring the police to report you and no further proof was needed. A whiff of alcohol on your breath was enough to get you locked up for 15 days.

I was sentenced as a Decembrist[5] when a neighbour reported me for banging on my door. I had lost my key and forgotten that Olga was at work. My trial lasted no more than a minute and the verdict was not subject to appeal. I did my time in a filthy police cell, deprived of tobacco and having to sleep on the bare floor.

On my release I was summoned to a workplace meeting and branded as a stain on the honour of the collective. Party demagogues and careerists had free rein. My mates sat solemnly through my denunciation, knowing that any one of them could have been standing in my shoes. They took me out for a drink afterwards to cheer me up.

In an attempt to humiliate us Decembrists the plant erected a bottle-shaped booth and a metal cup by its gates. We were paid our wages through a little window in the side of the bottle. We had to stand in the cup while the entire workforce of the plant filed past to the bus stop. Soon the bottle became a place where troikas

---

[5] Decembrists were revolutionaries sentenced in 1825 for plotting against Tsar Nicholas the First.

assembled before running to the nearest vodka shop.

'To hell with them all', I thought and sank even lower. I could see no reason to stop drinking. Life would be no better without the bottle. Shops would not suddenly fill with goods and the people around me would not blossom into interesting companions. I found a thousand convincing reasons to get drunk. If the house was clean and tidy, that had to be toasted; if Olga nagged me I had to register my protest. If someone had made a rude or untrue remark about me I drank to console my hurt feelings. When I felt misunderstood I drank. Most often it was my wife who was guilty of wounding my soul.

Each time I overstepped the mark I renounced the bottle for two or three months until my resolve crumbled. My periods of abstention convinced me that I could leave the bottle alone. Yet whether I was drinking or not I always had alcohol on my mind; I thought everyone had.

I missed so much work that my plant threatened me with the sack. Olga wanted me to have treatment but I protested.

"I drink no more than anyone else,"

"Then why don't you spend less time with your drinking partners and take a correspondance course? With a few qualifications you might get a more interesting position where you wouldn't want to waste all your time drinking."

"You must be mad if you think I'm going to spend my free time studying dialectical materialism," I told her, "just so I can swap my hammer and screwdriver for a phone and pen—and all for what? To win the right to bark at my friends? Anyway, you are a 'professional' but you earn less than me no matter how many abortions you perform."

"I sometimes wonder why I married you."

"Because if you had not, you would have had to repay your debt to the state by going to practise your medical skills on some godforsaken collective farm. Not even your Party Papa could have saved you from that fate."

In the end I agreed to seek treatment just to keep everyone quiet. Through her contacts Olga got me into a psychiatric clinic. Each day I was given three grammes of a drug called Antabuse, followed by 30-40 grammes of vodka. This cocktail took my breath away. I felt as though I was suffocating. They revived me with oxygen and gave me apomorphine, but not enough for my taste.

With Antabuse in my system I kept off the booze for eight months. During that period our daughter Daisy was born and I stayed at home caring for her while my wife worked night shifts.

'If only Mitya Karamazov and Nastasya Filipovna were my brother and sister,' I thought, 'how well we would understand each other and what wild times we would have!' Remembering my childhood admiration for Robinson Crusoe, I wondered why people in books were so much more interesting than those in real life.

I had been introduced to Dostoevsky's works by my uncle Dmitri Maslovski, who was married to my stepfather's sister, Aunt Ira. They lived at the Studioni Avrag dacha with their daughter. By that time the old folks were long dead. In the 1920s Uncle Dima had inherited a large house in the centre of Kuibyshev. The upkeep had proved too expensive so he sold it for the fabulous sum of half a million roubles. Thus the Maslovski family escaped poverty despite Uncle Dima's alcoholism.

After Daisy's birth my family and I went over to spend the summer at the dacha. One evening we were discussing literature over dinner and I dismissed Dostoevsky as wordy and dull. Without a word Uncle Dima went to the bookshelves and presented me with a set of ten volumes. I read them out of respect for my uncle, who had been rector of a college in the Ukraine. Those books opened my eyes: 'But people in the last century lived their daily lives just as we do!' I thought in astonishment, 'Marmeladov could be me!'

We spent the days mushroom-picking in the forest and swimming in the Volga. One cold and rainy evening at the end of summer we were having dinner when Aunt Ira made some thoughtless remark. Uncle Dima calmly rose from the table and walked out of the house leaving his coat behind. We continued to eat, thinking he had gone to the earth-closet at the end of the garden. As darkness fell I guessed something was wrong so I went out to look for him. I followed the path down to the river, past kitchen gardens that were already smelling of damp cabbages and decay. Reaching the river bank I turned and walked towards the light that burned in the river station ticket booth.

"Did Dmitri Maslovski come this way?" I asked the ticket-man, who knew everyone.

"Sure, he got on the Krasnaya Glinka bus about half an hour ago."

He was gone. I turned and went back to my family in the dacha.

"Ah, let the old devil come home in his own time," said Aunt Ira.

A few days later Uncle Dima phoned to say that he was safe but Aunt Ira was not to look for him.

Many years passed before their daughter found him in a flat belonging to a woman who had died not long beforehand. Uncle Dima had gone to the woman that night and she had taken him in. Hearing that Uncle Dima was alone, Aunt Ira asked him to return to Studioni Avrag. By that time he was blind and almost deaf. When I went to visit him I found him sitting on a wicker chair outside the dacha, paying no attention to the mosquitoes as he listened through a hearing aid to his transistor radio, his last link with the outside world.

"Uncle Dima," I shouted in his ear, "I want to thank you for introducing me to Dostoevsky."

Uncle Dima gave a smile of recognition.

I sat down next to him and continued: "You know, I admire Prince Mishkin even more than Don Quixote. Sometimes I think him higher than Christ, for he was no divine but human and fallible like the rest of us."

Uncle Dima nodded enthusiastically, "Of course the mushrooms haven't been so good this year," he shouted, "we need more rain."

I slipped four boxes of codeine into my socks and a hot-water bottle full of vodka into my waistband. Then I went into the prisoners' zone where my old friend Lyokha was waiting at a prearranged spot. He winked and slipped me some packets of sugar in return for my goodies. In town we did not see sugar for months on end, but the prisoners could buy it in their camp shop. On the other hand we could get as much codeine as we wanted from our chemists without prescription.

I thought Lyokha was unfortunate to have ended up behind barbed wire, but I felt no pity for the rest of the prisoners. I believed they must have done something to earn their sentences, although I did not blame them when they skived off work. No one likes working under the lash. There was nothing to distinguish the prisoners from the rest of us except their shaven heads. We were warned to be vigilant but that was unnecessary for they kept to themselves.

About half the inhabitants of Toliatti were former zeks[6] who were freed when Khrushchev revised the Criminal Code[7]. Ex-cons differed little from the rest of us. We all hated Party activists. Anyone who hobnobbed with bosses was regarded as a traitor. Perhaps in Moscow shop-floor workers drank with engineers and administrators but in the provinces bosses were our enemies. Those who crept after them were shunned by their workmates, leaving them with nothing else to do but build their careers.

Lyokha was released after he had served a year for hooliganism. Strangely enough, his wife left her policeman and returned to him. I asked Lyokha why this was.

"Simple, Vanya. My exceptional virility is instantly apparent to women, and not only to my wife, but doctors, singers, any woman at all. I only have to talk

---

[6] Zek—short form of zaklyuchennii: prisoner.
[7] The Soviet Criminal Code was revised in 1961.

to a tractor for five minutes and it starts to run after me."

"Vanya," Lyokha called one evening, "I'm on night shift. Bring a bottle over to the office and get out of your wife's hair."

I was only too happy to comply with his request. The local shop was already closed so I stopped off at a flat where Gypsies traded around the clock.

Lyokha had taken a job as a phone engineer. I arrived at his office and we downed the bottle between us. The vodka set me free. I forgot about my work, my wife and my leg. Just then it seemed that no one understood me better than Lyokha did.

"You know, Lyokha, I can't talk to Olga like I can to you. She is close to me, but after all, she is my wife. We know each other too well. I can guess what she is going to say even as she opens her mouth."

"I know. I stopped reading poems to Masha after she became my wife. But never mind, Vanya, listen to this," replied Lyokha, and handed me a set of headphones. He dialled a number.

"It's the director of Plant No. 2," he explained.

When a man's voice answered Lyokha said politely: "This is the telephone maintenance collective. How long is your telephone cord?"

We heard the idiot waking his wife and sending her to fetch a tape measure.

"Two and a half metres."

"Very good. Now pull out the cord and stick it up your arse."

Lyokha and I doubled up with laughter and hung up. At three in the morning, Lyokha called the director again and shouted down the line: "It's me! You can take it out now!"

Lyokha was soon dismissed from the phone collective. After that he returned to Chapaevsk, where he could only find work as a 'golden man', as we called those who scooped shit out of the barrack latrines.

I first met my friend Ivan Shirmanov at a works party, where he surprised me by drinking nothing at all. I had met teetotallers before but there was nothing priggish about Ivan. He played the accordion well and his anecdotes were unusually witty. I talked to him about my life in the Far East. He nodded, "I know the taiga; I was in Kolyma[8]."

Then one day Ivan stopped coming to work and our trade union sent me to find out what had happened to him. He lived in part of a pre-revolution wooden house. His sister Elizaveta timidly opened the door and ushered me into a gloomy, evil-smelling room. Empty bottles rolled around the floor. Ivan lay on an iron bedstead; its mattress was soaked through where he had wet himself.

"He needs a doctor, he can't stop drinking by himself," said his sister.

Ivan lay on his back, giggling mischievously.

"Elizaveta," he interjected, "you poor woman. You don't know how amusing it is to see everything floating before your eyes. Thoughts circle my head like butterflies. I cannot decide which one to snare. Each seems more fascinating than the last. I reach towards one,

---

[8] Kolyma was an area of camps in the Soviet Far East.

dwell upon it for an instant, and then it drifts off before I can secure it in my grasp. Oh, the devils!"

Ivan doubled up with laughter.

"Ivan, what should I do? Do you want to keep your job?" I asked, "If you leave it any longer they'll dismiss you for 'dishonourable reasons' and then you'll be portering for the rest of your life."

Silently he handed me a notice of resignation that he had already written out.

"You don't have to resign," I said, "we can come up with an excuse."

Ivan remained unmoved: "I want to leave without a fuss. This is my problem and I must sort it out myself."

Next day I told my workmates what had happened. They were a good bunch, none of them careerists or back stabbers, and we decided to pack the next trade union meeting to plead Ivan's case. It was forbidden to dismiss someone without the approval of their union and unions had to have the agreement of their members. When Ivan's dismissal was presented for approval I spoke up: "Comrades! Is it not our duty to help Comrade Shirmanov? As the advanced class the proletariat triumphed over the bourgeoisie, so can we not also triumph over alcoholism, not that there is really any such thing in the USSR? Let us return Comrade Shirmanov to the right path!"

Strangely enough, the meeting was swayed by my argument and the union even proposed to pay my fare to escort Ivan to a mental hospital. A Party man, Sashka Akulshina, accompanied us. Sashka had left his family behind in Chapaevsk while he arranged accommodation in Stavropol. His absence from his wife and his no-less-beloved Party organisation led him into strong temptation. When Ivan suggested going by bus instead of taxi Sashka readily agreed. After all, we were economising the money that the work collective had contributed to the return of the prodigal son. By the time we reached the clinic the doctors could not tell who was bringing in whom for treatment. I only recognised the hospital by the slogan on its outside wall: *Let us wage war on Drunkenness!*

Despite our efforts Ivan never came back to work in our plant. He took portering jobs and his sister continued to look after him. He was the only one of my friends to whom my wife would lend money, although she knew quite well what he wanted it for.

"If I don't lend it him poor Elizaveta will," she said.

One day Ivan and I went out in search of good beer. The only bar that sold it was on the steamer that plied between Moscow and Astrakhan. We boarded the boat, went to the restaurant and bought up all the beer they had. Then we sat back and enjoyed the swaying of the craft on the wide expanses of the Volga. Our plan was to sail as far as Sengilei and take the bus home. The journey should have taken us three hours. We returned home three days later. We had woken up in Kazan, with our pockets empty and Ivan's shoes gone. We returned downriver on rafts, like Huckleberry Finn. The raft people, who ferried logs down from the northern forests to Volga cities, laughed when they heard our story and let us ride for nothing. Ivan entertained them on the way with his jokes. In that way I learned that it is possible to live without a house and to travel without money.

I felt as though a reindeer herd had spent the night in my mouth, my head spun and my thoughts crawled away from my grasp. With shaking hands I gathered my clothes and tiptoed into the kitchen to dress. I tried to smoke the first cigarette of the day without vomiting. I knew I would not be able to go to work unless I had a hair-of-the-dog. A little pile of coins was stacked on the window-sill. I took it and crept out of the house while the others slept. That night I came home in a happy mood to find Olga waiting for me in a rage.

"That was the last of our money. I put it aside to buy milk for Daisy," she spat.

I would not let her see how bad I felt.

"What the hell do you want, Olga? Okay, I drink, but no more than anyone else. You can't say I am a bad husband—I even help you with the washing for Christ's sake—and I don't chase women."

"Just as well. Who would want a drunk like you?"

"And you don't see me out in the courtyard all day with the domino players. I don't go on fishing trips."

"If it weren't for your leg you'd be off like a shot with your rod and bottles."

I could not bear to be reminded of my leg. I left for the hostel that night.

There I unburdened myself to my friends. "The trouble with Olga is that she thinks she knows better than me because she has a degree. It's a mistake to marry a woman more educated than yourself."

I got the sympathy I craved from men who were in a similar position to mine. I moved into the hostel and life became a long drinks party, with a little work thrown in for good measure.

Olga found me outside the vodka shop waiting for my hair-of-the-dog. "Vanya, come with me," she said, "I've got an invitation to Professor Burenkov's clinic in Chelyabinsk. He's developed a new treatment. It's banned by Moscow so it probably works."

I did not protest as I was beginning to tire of life in the hostel. Olga took me home, gave me something to help me sleep, and in the morning we took a train to the Urals.

At the clinic we joined 25 other men, each accompanied by his wife or mother. We introduced ourselves. I was surprised to see the alcoholics were not all ordinary working men like me. There was a surgeon who confessed he had once been so drunk that he had fallen on top of a patient on the operating table. Next to me sat a Hero of the Soviet Union, with medals on his jacket but no shirt under it; he had sold his clothes for a drink. Professor Burenkov said to him: "Well, you defeated the fascists but you allowed vodka to defeat you."

The Hero looked sheepish.

First Burenkov gave us each a bitter herb drink, then a massive dose of Antabuse. Next we had to down a glass of vodka. The Antabuse reacted badly with the vodka and soon we were vomiting and writhing in pain. It is hard to see two dozen men retch and groan all around you without feeling dreadful yourself. I thought I was going to die. Professor Burenkov strode around the group roaring: "Anyone want another drink?"

The relatives outside were excitedly watching the drama through a window, beating on the glass and cheering: "Give them more vodka!"

Burenkov injected us with camphor and made us lie on mattresses with our left arms above our heads in order not to strain our hearts. Later he took us all outside. We sat under trees, feeling life return. The doctor showed us slides of swollen livers and the abnormal brains of children of alcoholics. That night we took our trains home, clutching our supplies of Antabuse.

As Burenkov's popularity grew throughout the country he stopped practising. An unknown number of people died after anxious wives and mothers slipped Antabuse into food. It had no smell or taste so alcoholics consumed it unknowingly and then choked to death after they had had a few drinks. Women usually administered the Antabuse in good faith—they were simply desperate to keep their menfolk out of prison.

Before I went to Burenkov it had looked as though my days at the factory were numbered. After my cure the administration were so impressed that they put me in charge of the factory's credit fund. This fund was designed to help us buy expensive items such as fridges. It was usually controlled by a group of women supervisors who borrowed all they wanted while telling shop-floor workers that the funds had run out. They said we only wanted the money to buy vodka. The director dismissed the women and placed me in charge. After that every alcoholic in the plant came to me for three roubles for his troika session.

Now I was sober my thoughts tormented me and prevented me from sleeping. To calm me down my wife prescribed the popular Hungarian barbiturate Noxiron. At first two or three of these tablets were enough to knock me out but my need soon grew. I dropped in on

Olga at work and discreetly tore off some blank prescription forms from her pad. I could fill them out without trouble as I knew the Latin alphabet. Her signature was as indecipherable as any other doctor's and easy to forge. Having written out several prescriptions I went around to different chemists in the area, acquiring enough Noxiron to last a month.

Olga noticed that I was taking a lot of barbiturate and tried to explain that my new addiction was as harmful as the old one. To appease her I stopped taking the tablets during the day but at night I swallowed them until I passed out.

I shared my discovery with my former drinking partners who, like me, had had to choose between alcohol and their wives and jobs. One day when Olga was away my friends came over for a Noxiron session. My wife returned to find me sprawled on the floor, black and blue with bruises. When I tried to stand up I toppled over like a felled tree. I could not even extend my hands to break my fall. The rubbish bin was full of Noxiron packaging. Olga put me to bed.

That evening a colleague of my wife's and her husband came to tea. I dragged myself out of bed to join them. With relief I remembered I had some pills left. Excusing myself, I went into the corridor where my coat was hanging and began to rummage in its pockets.

"You won't find what you are looking for." Olga stood in the doorway, pointing to the toilet. My hopes of avoiding horrific withdrawal symptoms were dashed.

"Bitch! You had no right to go through my pockets!"

Olga walked away. I followed her into the room, still raging. With one blow I swept the glass jam dish off the table. The jam splattered over our lady guest's new cardigan and the dish smashed the glass of our book-cabinet.

The lady's husband led me into the kitchen. We smoked and I calmed down a little. When we went back into the living-room I saw my wife putting Daisy's things into an overnight bag. Everyone left.

I found a bottle of vodka that had been put aside for some family celebration. Although I had been taking Antabuse for several months I opened the bottle and began to drink. I soon passed out.

In the morning the doorbell rang. Expecting my wife, I opened the door and a policeman entered. "You are under arrest," he said and walked calmly through into the living room. There he sat down at the table and began to fill in a form. I went into the kitchen and drank the remaining vodka in one gulp. After that it was all the same to me whether the policeman took me off to a health spa or to a leper colony.

chapter four

"A year! You could sit that out on the shit bucket!"

My cell mates in Syzran jail thought I had got off lightly for menacing society with malicious hooliganism of a particularly vicious form.

Olga visited me after the trial. "Vanya," she pleaded, "I never expected them to send you to prison. I tried to withdraw my statement but they threatened to give me two years for laying false charges. And you heard the judge . . . "

At the trial she had wept and asked them not to punish me, but the judge told her to shut up.

"Perhaps he was right," I said sternly. "If every wife was allowed to change her mind trials all over the country would collapse and there would be chaos."

We had nothing left to say to each other. If I told Olga what I thought of her she would walk away thinking I deserved to be in prison. "Don't worry about me," I said, "It makes a change to be living here. The company is delightful."

I babbled on about prison life until it was time for her to go. Olga threw me a despairing look as she left.

Waiting for the trial had been the worst part; now that I knew how long my sentence would be I settled down to await my transfer to a labour camp. I can't say I felt depressed; I was curious about my fellow inmates and interested to find out what camp life would be like.

In the jail we were housed in long barrack huts that we called cowsheds. As new prisoners came in they talked about what they had done. One or two swore they would never again pick up a knife or a glass of vodka, but most thought their arrival in prison was pure misfortune. They rarely saw any justice in their sentence and were sure it would be their last.

The boy in the bunk next to mine was an exception. Vovik was a country lad of 18 who had been sentenced for robbing village stores. "A thief's life is the best of all," he said, "I want no other. Robbing those stores was like shooting fish in a barrel; they don't have alarms. We found out beforehand where the money was kept. The assistants left the takings in the shop overnight because they did not trust their husbands. After we had helped ourselves a few times we went to the Black Sea for a holiday."

"What did you do there?" I asked.

"We ate ice cream until we burst and went to the cinema as often as we liked. The trouble was, as we changed the notes we had stolen our pockets became so weighted down with coins that our trousers hung off our arses. One night in the park we dropped all our loose change onto a flowerbed. Unfortunately a policeman noticed and grew suspicious. He pulled us in and one of my mates broke under interrogation. We each got three years.

"What is the point of stealing a few roubles just to get caught and end up inside like this?" I asked.

"I never saw ice cream on the collective farm; in Sochi I ate it day and night. Stealing is easy; I shall take it up again as soon as they let me out."

Vovik spent his time drawing elaborate ballpoint churches on handkerchieves. Prisoners soaked these and pressed them to their backs, leaving delicate tracings which were then tattooed into the skin. Vovik's churches were very popular and he had orders from other cells besides ours. He was a good-natured boy, willing to share out country foodstuffs sent in by grateful village shop assistants, along with knitted gloves, socks and scarves.

"I'm carrying the can for them," he explained. "They all have their hands in the till too."

I welcomed the odd scrap from Vovik's parcels. I refused the food my wife sent in but it was hard to exist on prison rations. In the morning we were issued half a loaf of clay-like bread which had to last the whole day. Taking a tip from the old lags, I tried not to gobble up my bread at once but to keep some to chew in the evening. This was important. Those who ate theirs all at once spent the whole day looking at the others' bread with hungry eyes. Some men developed an insatiable desire for food, begging it from the other zeks.

'That's how you lose your self respect,' I thought.

I had hardly got used to prison routine in Syzran when the shout came one morning to pack up our things and assemble outside. We were marched through town to the station. I followed on behind in a cart with four women prisoners. My leg prevented me from keeping up with the men.

At the station we were surrounded by snarling alsatians straining at their chains. With kicks and cuffs the guards made us sit on the floor. Townspeople and travellers milled about but no one stood and gawped. Men casually reached into their pockets as they passed and threw us cigarettes. An old lady pushed past the guards and silently placed a bundle of pies on a prisoner's lap.

From the outside our 'Stolypin' carriage looked no different to a normal passenger car except that there were no windows on one side. Each compartment held about twenty men, and was sectioned off from the corridor by steel bars. Experienced prisoners made straight for the top bunk and kicked off anyone who tried to follow them. We had no idea where we were going. Finally, when the train started to move we learned our destination was to be a camp near Tashkent.

Our bread and herring rations made us desperately thirsty. The guards gave out very little water for they could not be bothered to escort us to the toilet. "Have patience lads," said an elderly zek, "the suffering will pass. Salt absorbs water, so if you eat the herring you won't sweat so much; you'll hold water in your bodies."

As the train pulled into Saratov news came through that an earthquake had destroyed most of Tashkent. We were diverted to Astrakhan. When we reached that city I was squeezed into a Black Maria with 32 others. A prisoner lost consciousness in the stifling van. No one took any notice of our cries for help. The old zek raised his voice: "Okay lads, start rocking."

We leaned first to one side of the van and then the other. The vehicle began to tilt dangerously and the drivers stopped. The guards unloaded the sick man and sent him to hospital. Then they punished us by taking away our tobacco.

"We once derailed a train this way," said the old man. "When you are looking at 25 years hard labour you don't care what you do."

Corrective Labour Camp No. 4 held people who had committed crimes against the person. The camp was so near the town that at night we could hear trolleybuses rattling past. In the daytime we worked in an industrial zone making prefab homes for the virgin lands of Siberia.

While we were waiting to be processed the elderly zek from the Black Maria explained the nature of the camp.

"It's a bitches zone[1]," he said, "although there haven't been any here for a long while. However there are a lot of goats[2]. Most of them are SVPs[3]."

Almost half the inmates wore SVP armbands. They helped to keep internal order. If for example, an SVP saw someone smoking in an unauthorised place, but the guards were taking no notice, he would run to the watch and point it out.

Recruitment for the SVP was carried out by the 'Godfather', the prison MVD officer. He interviewed everyone, explaining that only members of the SVP got remission and other concessions. When he invited me to join I thought it best not to tell him what I thought of SVPs, so I tried to convince him of my unsuitability for the role.

---

[1] Bitches were renegade thieves-by-code (a criminal caste who were not allowed to work, marry, own property or accumulate money. All stolen goods had to be pooled. When arrested they were not allowed to cooperate with the authorities in any way). From the 1920s onward the Soviet regime set out to destroy this old criminal underworld. Some thieves-by-code gave in under torture and agreed to cooperate with the authorities. In the 1950s special planeloads of these bitches, MVD agents among them, were flown from one camp to another where they fought for control.

If the authorities placed a thief-by-code in a bitches zone he would kill the first person he came across in order to get a transfer. When the death penalty was reintroduced the camp wars quietened down. By the late 1960x thieves-by-code no longer existed except in Georgia. Their successors were known as thieves of the western type, who ran organised crime and illicit business. These criminals formed the Russian mafia and the old type of thief disappeared.

[2] Goats were either informers or witnesses for the prosecution.

[3] SVPs were an internal camp police force recruited from the prisoners,

"A condition of my sentence is that I am treated for alcoholism."

"We don't have such facilities in this camp."

"And I am to serve my full sentence, so what's the point of joining the SVP?"

The Godfather let me go.

I had not become a Pioneer leader in my youth and I was not about to start telling tales now. Our teachers had wanted to create a nation of stool pigeons, but fortunately not everyone had listened to them. It was the same in camp: the rest of us despised SVPs as the lowest form of human life.

I noticed that two SVPs in my cell had agreed to share all the extra food they received from parcels and bonuses. When their locker was full one of them hid a razor blade in the other's bed and told the guard about it. A search party found the blade, that man got ten days in the isolator and his friend ate all the food. That incident taught me a lot about the SVPs' mentality.

Those who worked and met their quotas received a small amount of money with which to buy goods in the camp shop. Anything unfit for sale in Astrakhan's stores came to us: piles of stuck-together sweets, dirty sugar, stinking herring and gritty rusks. The shop also sold rough shag tobacco for 6 kopecks a packet. Vodka and tea came in via civilian workers in the industrial zone. They would bribe the guards to look the other way.

On my arrival I went straight to the camp trader and offered my change of underwear for a very low price. Then I was able to buy enough tobacco to last me until my first pay. I would not have to humble myself by begging for it from other prisoners. Another prisoner said, "Idiot! You sold a new pair of pants and a vest for two roubles!"

"The idiot was the one who bought them. He paid for rags and I bought independence!"

The next morning new arrivals were assembled for work detail. One of the camp officers asked, "Is there anyone here who has completed their secondary education?"

I stepped forward.

"You will help in the library," the officer said.

I was lucky to get such a cushy job. In the morning I handed out letters and in the evening prisoners came for books and newspapers. 'Soviet Woman' was especially popular. Pictures of pretty women adorned walls and lockers. The prisoners replaced them as soon as the guards tore them down.

My days would have passed easily enough, had it not been for the camp storekeeper, a former colonel, who kept dropping into the library to plague me. This man destroyed any lingering respect I might have had for epaulettes: only in Russia could such an utterly stupid man have risen to such a high rank. His self confidence was so absolute it shocked me. He showed me the book he was writing; *Life is not a Bed of Roses* described his life from birth to prison camp. In his childhood he had been the top student, he ran the fastest and jumped the highest. In his youth he had been more handsome and intelligent than his peers, in the army braver than his comrades-in-arms. His wife had been the regimental beauty; he had killed her from jealousy.

Our literary journals had already rejected the first

volume of the colonel's work; he assumed this was because it contained grammatical errors. Now he wanted my help with corrections. I tried to excuse myself, saying I was not very literate, but he was so insistent I had to agree. The task oppressed me but I had not the courage to tell the colonel the truth.

A fellow prisoner named Oleg came to my rescue. He was an intelligent lad who had dropped out of university. We became friends and spent all our free time together. He helped me proof-read the colonel's book and we laughed over it together.

The library was stocked with classics and Dostoevsky's works were constantly borrowed, especially *Crime and Punishment*. But the zeks were only attracted by the title. and returned the book disillusioned, having been unable to understand its archaic language. I tried to warn them in advance, for I do not believe that someone of 40 can suddenly become converted to Dostoevsky.

I was puzzled by the fact that the correspondance of our greatest authors was in constant demand. I had read Blok's letters and had been disappointed—and I was more educated than most. One prisoner after another came up to borrow Turgenev's letters to Pauline Viardot. Old editions of local papers were also in heavy demand. Finally Oleg explained the mystery:

"Until last year petitioners for divorce had to make an announcement in their local papers. For example: *Citizeness Ivanovna, Anna Semyonova, born 1942, living at 5, Sadovaya Street, has initiated divorce proceedings* . . .

"Prisoners note down the names and addresses of divorced women and then they copy out Turgenev's letters. Imagine how citizeness Ivanovna feels. She is alone after kicking out the husband who sold all her furniture for drink. Suddenly she receives a letter from an unknown admirer! And written in such effusive language that it makes her head spin. She replies and thus she becomes what we call an external student. Yura and Fedka each have three external students. They sometimes get parcels. There is a woman in our street at home who married a prisoner after she became his external student."

"But can't they see from our address that this is a camp?"

"The zeks say they are working in a secret military plant, which is why the address is just a number. I am sure many women guess the truth but all the same they continue to write. It is better to receive a letter than nothing at all. Remember the joke about two women friends who meet each other in the street? One says: 'How's the old man, drinking?'

'Yes, the parasite.'

'Knocking you around?'

'Yes, the bastard.'

'Well, you can't complain, at least he's in good health.'"

I laughed. Being a married woman in the 'happiest' country in the world was better than being divorced, widowed or single. "Don't you have an external student?" I asked Oleg.

"I don't need one. My own wife is enough. She had me arrested for domestic violence. She pleaded for clemency at the trial but the judge was unmoved.

"Lily was the most beautiful girl in town," Oleg continued, "but everyone despised her because she had been born in prison. Her mother came from the Moscow intelligentsia and her father was an army officer of Polish origin. He was shot after the war as a cosmopolitan. After her release from jail Lily's mother was given a minus 20[4], so she ended up in Astrakhan.

"Lily's mother was a proud and defiant woman. The locals said she was a prostitute. They were suspicious of a single mother coming out of prison, especially as she was a member of the intelligentsia. Lily was an aggressive child, always hanging around with the boys and baiting the teachers. She would start a fight for the slightest reason and she often won, despite her size.

"Soon after they locked me up Lily had a baby. When she wants to see me she comes to the camp, sets our daughter down on the threshold of the director's office and runs away. Then she phones up and demands my release. The baby screeches like a stuck pig, the guards can do nothing with her and in the end they give us a special visit. Then Lily takes the child away until the next time she decides she wants a visit. If it was within the director's personal powers I'd probably be free by now."

The library was separated from the camp schoolroom by a thin partition. School was compulsory for all those under 60 who had not completed the seventh class. Those who refused had parcels and visits withheld. Teachers were civilian volunteers. The sound of these lessons kept Oleg and me entertained as we worked.

---

[4] A minus 20 meant she was prohibited from living in the 20 largest cities in the USSR.

"Masha goes to the shop," the teacher's voice read out one day.

Some wit remarked: "It would be better if the bitch came to see us."

Ignoring him the teacher's voice continued: "Who can tell me which is the subject of the sentence?"

Silence.

"You, Kuznetsov, come up to the board, please."

"What's the point if I don't know the fucking answer?" replied Kuznetsov, but we heard the scrape of his bench as he rose.

"Which word is the subject of the sentence?"

After some thought Kuznetsov answered: "Er, Masha?"

"Correct! and which is the verb?"

"Um, 'shop'?"

"No. Who can say?"

"Of course it is 'goes' but we would say: 'staggers'" another voice piped up.

"How do you mean 'staggers'?" asked the teacher.

"Well, Masha has obviously got a hangover and is going for a bottle."

"No not, 'staggers' but 'waddles', because of the huge arse on her."

At that point everyone threw themselves into an impassioned discussion about Masha's qualities and failings, her physique and her temperament.

When exams took place candidates spilled out of the classroom into the library looking for us. Together we helped them solve problems and corrected their written mistakes. The teacher did not try to stop us. The more who passed the better it looked for him.

Our camp had a technical school which was supposed to give inmates skills that would deter them from the path of crime. The yard outside the school was full of farm machinery waiting to be repaired. It was protected from the weather by tarpaulin and guarded by an old man who had been sentenced for killing his wife. In her death struggle she had hit him so hard on the head with an iron that he had a dent in his cranium the size of a fist. The blow had altered his mind.

Oleg and I approached the old man one day: "Look here, Grandad," said Oleg, "It's a pity to sit here all day doing nothing. If you cut this tarpaulin into strips and sew them together you'll be able to make a balloon. We'll bring you some rope; you'll tie your balloon to your chair, and then you'll be able to float out of here. If you leave on a moonless night no one will see you. We won't say anything. It'll be a secret between the three of us."

The old man was excited by the plan and for a whole month he busily sewed together pieces of tarpaulin. He was eventually caught, but by this time he had taken to sewing. One day he turned up on evening parade in a marshall's uniform, sewn from tarpaulin bleached white by the sun, and covered in stripes and tin medals made from old fish cans. We cheered as he smartly saluted the camp guards.

It was hard to get used to the camp regime, with endless searches and body counts. For hours we had to stand like sheep in the rain or snow. The semi-literate guards lined us up in fives; even so, they were always losing count and having to start again.

Those who wanted to get out of work would cut

their wrists or nail their scrotums to their bunks. When a man in our cell slashed his wrists with a piece of smuggled razor I wanted to call the guards. Oleg shrugged and said, "Don't be in a hurry; death holds no fear when the world looks on."

And it was true; no one died of a few slashes across their wrists. They did it for show, out of hysteria.

A prisoner named Kuptsev was an exception. He would regularly hide somewhere in the basement or under the roof, slit his wrists and wait for someone to find him. He never sought help himself. When I asked him why he did it he said, "The sensation of blood draining out of my body is like nothing else in the world."

I once saw a man just after he had cut his stomach open. He stood smiling in front of the guards, with his dripping guts cupped in his hands. Stories of people who cut themselves up are usually told with a grin but they are not funny. Everyone responds to cruelty and injustice in their own way.

In prison and camp I found the lack of solitude even harder to bear than the loss of freedom. You are always in a crowd. This is not so bad when you are working during the daytime, but at night you sleep among hundreds of men whose faces you have tired of a long while ago. You start to hate your fellow inmates and they you.

In the beginning I was surprised to see zeks turn on warders for no apparent reason, insulting them and getting punished for it. Then I started to do the same thing myself, just to gain some solitude in the isolator.

In the evenings we exercised by shuffling around a small square. By unspoken agreement the walkers did not disturb each other. If you paced up and down for long enough you started to feel almost light headed and detached from your surroundings. For a minute or two you could forget you were in a camp. Returning from one of these evening shuffles a tall Jew named Yura Kots approached me and remarked casually: "Wine drinkers smell different in the morning."

"So they do," I replied, "But what makes you say so?"

"This is going to be the first sentence of the novel that I shall write when I get out of here."

"Do you know the joke about the madman who spent all day writing?"

"Tell me. I could do with a laugh."

"A doctor came up to him and asked: 'What are you writing?'"

"'A letter', he replied."

"'Who to?'"

"'Myself.'"

"'And what does it say?'"

"'How should I know? I'll find out when I get it.'"

"But I really am going to write a novel," said Kots.

"When?"

"When I leave here."

After that Kots and I began to take our shuffles beside each other. Each month he received a parcel of books which he passed on to me when he had finished. In the evenings we discussed our readings and studied German together.

By profession Kots was a card sharp, but he had been sent to camp for theft. One day he lost to more experienced players. A card debt is a very serious matter. In order to repay it Kots robbed his former college. He was caught trying to make off with a tape recorder and given three years.

I was surprised to see that Kots subscribed to 'Young Communist.'

"What's up, need extra bog paper?" I asked.

"No."

"Then why do you order that rubbish?"

"There are a lot of things written here that you won't find anywhere else."

He showed me some notes on the last page about a debate between Sartre and Camus. This had taken place a few years ago but everything went through the USSR like a giraffe's neck, and Kots had to keep up-to-date on western literature in order to maintain his pose as an intellectual.

Kots used to tour the country, presenting himself now as an architect, now as a doctor. He met his victims on long-distance trains or on the beaches of health spas. While he was swindling someone at cards he would remark casually to his victim: "Of course, as Camus was not really an existentialist . . . "

Marcel Proust was Kots' trump card, deadlier than a Kalashnikov in his hands. The credulous intelligentsia, who thought that intellect was something you picked up with your university degree, were impressed. Kots would quickly empty his opponents' pockets and then disappear.

Although I admired Kots and envied him his freedom I never thought of following his example. A life of crime seemed too complicated and if I was honest, I knew it was beyond my capabilities. Besides, it would inevitably lead me back to prison. I had never held romantic notions about the brotherhood of thieves. They only band together when it is profitable to do so or when they are afraid. It is not hard to give away what has been easily come by, so thieves are accustomed to dividing up their booty. However, when it comes down to parting with their last it is a very different story. When they are in difficulties thieves display as much soldarity as spiders in a jar.

No one in my family had been to prison before me. I did not count my father. Those were different times. Besides, that was for a 'political crime'. By the 1960s political crimes were not regarded as crimes at all, although at home people tried to keep their distance from former political prisoners, 'to keep away from sin' they said.

Even though I was not attracted to a life of crime I would not condemn my fellow inmates. It took me two weeks behind barbed wire to learn not to judge others. When I was first locked up I had held myself a little aloof from the other prisoners. I figured that they were probably inside for a reason while I had only been put away through a misunderstanding. But I soon realised that most of the prisoners were just like me. If you excluded the murderers, bandits and professional thieves, I could have stood in the shoes of any one of them. It was only through some happy accident that I had not been thrown into prison before. I could have been locked up just for all the spirit I had stolen from work.

In the course of my life I have read masses of camp literature written by former political prisoners, and I must say that it is dishonest of them to paint the criminal zeks in the blackest of colours, as many do. In the first place, we are all human beings; in the second, we are not all the same.

Everyone in the Soviet Union stole. Wages were calculated on the expectation that people would do so—just for their own survival. Collective farmers worked for years without seeing any money at all; they would have died out like the mammoth if they had not stolen.

This was no accident. Every member of a gang has to dirty his hands with a crime, so our government deliberately pushed people towards committing them. If someone then turns round and complains about the system, who is going to listen to him if his hands are already dirty?

In fact, most prisoners are in jail not for what they have done, but for the time and place of their appearance on this earth. I have to thank God that I was born in 1935 and not 15 years earlier. My long tongue would surely have earned me a bullet in the head during the 1930s repression.

I was released in December, after exactly a year. Oleg had to stay inside for another three months. We arranged to keep in touch. His mother and sister met me at the camp gate and saw me off on a flight to Kuibyshev. I did not intend to go back to my wife. I could not forgive her for 365 days and nights behind barbed wire.

chapter five

"Ahh, Christ just walked barefoot through my heart!"

Ivan Shirmanov tossed back his first drink of the morning. We were toasting my freedom with a renewed sense of brotherhood.

"Thousands of books have been written about prisons," said Ivan, "but everyone's experience is unique, especially their first. It has been likened to first love, but in the case of love there are doubts: will there be a second? In the case of prison there are no doubts. There will be another and another and another..."

When we had finished the bottle we wandered down to the market-place, picking up more vodka on the way. There were a few alkashi[1] gathered there. Beaming all over his moonlike face, Ivan offered them a bottle. His expression as he watched them drink was that of a mother spooning porridge into her child's mouth.

Ivan introduced me to one of the group: "This is our Levanevsky, who is nothing like his famous namesake[2]. You can always trust him with cash to go and buy a bottle."

Levanevsky only took one glass from us.

"Have another?" I offered.

"I don't want any more," he replied, "God is no lovesick swain blinded by his passion. He sees everything. So long as he knows I'm trying he'll give me another chance to sort myself out."

I knew that in an hour he would be shaking and feeling like death.

In the market we came across Sedoy the Poet of All Russia. He was standing on an old lady's sunflower seed stall and declaiming to passing shoppers:

---

[1] Alkash (plural: alkashi): street-drinker, wino.
[2] In the 1930s a Soviet pilot called Levanevsky disappeared while flying over the newly-opened Arctic. His plane was never discovered. It became customary to say, 'he's done a Levanevsky' when someone disappeared without trace.

> *"Through Stavropol, unrecognised,*
> *I wander as a shadow.*
> *And I practise onanism*
> *On International Women's Day!"*

"Sedoy was once a teacher," said Ivan, "a head of department. His students nicknamed him Crocodile. Then he took to drink. His mother looks after him. Every day you see him in the market in a clean shirt and freshly-pressed trousers."

"There are a lot of alkashi like Sedoy," said Ivan. "As former members of the intelligentsia they blame society for their condition. They think it owes them something. A worker like me would be ashamed to beg or steal; I'll take any portering job I can find."

Amongst the alkashi I met former teachers, doctors, and engineers. No one respected them for their education; respect was earned by not stealing drinks and not always having your hair-of-the-dog at another's expense. When a person trembles from a hangover it is no great sin to cadge a drink, but the man who does this every morning soon annoys his companions. When alkashi notice that someone is trying to take advantage of them they spit in his face and drive him away. Outcasts can be seen hanging around the fringes of alkash groups, usually sporting black eyes.

The majority of alkashi tried to live at the expense of those around them. 'There are enough fools in this world to be taken advantage of,' they thought, and the more people they conned the better pleased with themselves they were. Even more degraded were those for whom life had no meaning at all. They lived only from one drink to the next. If you sent them for vodka they would disappear; if you drank with them they would go through your pockets when you passed out and probably treat you to a bottle over the head as well. One man who did this to me had the front to come up the following day, look into my eyes and ask, "How come we lost each other yesterday?"

Perhaps he really remembered nothing. I could not swear it was he who had hit me. I had been too drunk to catch him by the hand to look into his face.

The pay I had collected from camp soon ran out and I had to look for a job. That meant sobering up. I knew that if I went on sleeping at Ivan's I would soon be led into temptation, so I went to an old friend's flat. Igor Gorbunov came from the northern Urals where the people speak so fast it's hard to understand them. Like me, he loved reading, but unlike me he was no drunkard and in the past he had helped Olga extricate me from drinking parties.

Igor had visitors and they were preparing to go camping in the forest. I declined an invitation to join them as I knew they would be taking bottles with them. They set off, leaving me alone in the flat. I sat on the balcony with a book. Across the street was a vodka shop. Troikas were forming at the entrance, pooling their money and sending in one of their number to buy a bottle. It was nearly closing time and sales were speeding up. I needed cigarettes so I went down to the shop and joined the surging crowd of men around the counter. Pushing through with my elbows, I held out my money amongst the forest of hands.

"Cigarettes!"

"How many?" the assistant asked.

"Two packets."

She frowned at the amount I handed her and moved towards the till for change To save her the journey I involuntarily added: "And three bottles."

I could have left the bottles on the counter but that would have looked foolish in front of all those people. 'Well, I can always give them to an acquaintance outside,' I reasoned, but I did not know any of the men who were milling around the shop. So I returned to Igor's flat armed to the teeth, put the bottles in his fridge and sat down on the balcony with my book. As I tried to read the image of those bottles kept floating into my mind, breaking my concentration. Almost without thinking, I put the book aside, stood up, went through the living room into the kitchen and sidled over to the fridge.

The first glassful was hard to swallow. I retched but managed to force it down. After a while my throat relaxed and the mouthfuls fluttered down gently like little birds. Having seen off the first bottle, I felt the need of an audience: 'I can't call on his neighbours even with these two bottles,' I thought, 'they hardly know me.' Instead I wandered down to the yard. I recognised the metal spaceship in the children's play area. It had been remodelled from the Decembrist bottle that used to stand at the factory gates. A drunken tune emanated from the spaceship. It called to me like a siren song. Next morning I awoke in the dust without money, documents or shoes.

Olga opened the door: "I've been expecting you."

Silently I entered and cleaned myself up. For a few days we barely spoke and I kept out of her way. Finally she could bear it no longer.

"Vanya," she said, "it is my fault you went to prison, but you can't feel sorry for yourself all your life. Make up your mind. Either we divorce, or you put it all behind you."

My resentment boiled over: "Thanks to you I was stuck in that hole for a year. Can you imagine the endless searches and body counts, or what it is like to sit down to dinner with a man who has murdered his mother and another who has raped a three year old girl? To have the biggest idiot in the province shout at you for no reason when you cannot answer back? You know what the worst thing about camp is? That you are never alone for one minute. Sometimes I felt like commiting murder myself.

"You put me through all that and now you want me to behave as though nothing happened. And don't threaten me with divorce. I know you have nowhere to go. You won't humiliate yourself again by going back to your parents."

"All right, I made a mistake, but you can't use that to justify your behaviour forever. You use your anger with me as an excuse to drink, but in truth you drink because you are a coward. You can't face work, or me, or even poor Daisy. If you can stop blaming me, I am willing to support you until you get paid."

But prison has put an unbridgeable gulf between us. I felt as though I had crossed a boundary beyond which there could be no return to normal life. Olga would never understand what I had been through, and she was mistaken if she thought I could rebuild a life with her as though nothing had happened.

The factory told me I could start in the new year. I filled in the time by hanging around with my alkashi friends, who listened to my camp stories with sympathy and even admiration. Their attention stoked my self pity, and I began to enjoy my role as sufferer. The realisation of this fact did not make me proud of myself, so I submerged myself ever more deeply in drink.

One morning I crawled home to find the flat empty. Olga had taken almost everything that belonged to her and Daisy. 'She's trying to teach me a lesson,' I thought. 'I won't react.' After a week I phoned her work and they told me that she had resigned. 'That can't be true, for she has nowhere to go,' I thought.

Olga had left no money, so I sold the furniture, including my precious East German bookcase. I hauled it downstairs at five in the morning, tied it to Daisy's sledge and dragged it to the market. Alas, while I was taking a smoke break the wind turned my bookcase over and its beautiful glass doors were smashed. With great difficulty I converted it into a bottle, which my customer helped me drink.

In the end I sold the only living thing left in the flat, Daisy's hedgehog Yashka. The poor thing was hungry, as there was no food in the house. I took it to the shop *Nature*, not really hoping for money. I thought that at least someone might take it home for their children, but the shop assistant gave me one rouble and seventeen kopecks for Yashka. She knew the price of a bottle.

Finally I went to my wife's sister Ludmilla, who told me that Olga and Daisy were fine. They were living in a small mining town, they had found a flat and Daisy was going to a modern kindergarten. Ludmilla had promised not to disclose their whereabouts. That was the only information I could glean, but I felt calmer. Any decision I took would have to be made with a sober head, so I went home to sleep.

For two days I did not leave the house. Although there was a bottle of vodka in the kitchen I did not touch it. As each hour passed I felt worse. I could not sleep for a minute. The radio bothered me and so I switched it off, lay down and read. There was a snow storm outside; the wind rattled the window. On the third night I heard breaking glass outside. 'Bad luck,' I thought, thinking that someone had forgotten to shut their ventilation window and it had blown open and shattered.

Suddenly the doorbell rang. I went to answer it. On the threshhold stood my neighbour Voronin in his underpants. He was holding a gun, a 16 calibre rifle.

"Was it you who broke my window?" he asked.

"What? Are you crazy?"

"Show me your balcony," he demanded, and walked past me into the living-room.

Our balcony was next to his bedroom window. He tried the glass door but it would not open because of the snow piled against it.

"I thought you had gone out onto your balcony and broken my window with a mop," said Voronin.

"What would I want to do that for?" I asked, bewildered.

"Well who the hell knows what goes on in your mind, you've been pissed for two months," he snapped, and went home.

If I had stepped onto the balcony there would have been footprints in the snow, and there were none. Something was not right. Why would I break his window? I scarcely knew Voronin. He was the head doctor in the clinic where Olga worked. We exchanged greetings on the stairs and his wife sometimes borrowed matches. There was no quarrel between us. After thinking hard about the incident I went to fetch a hammer and six inch nail. I nailed the balcony door shut. Let them say what they like now! But the business still worried me. And a gun!

The more I thought about it the more convinced I was that some sort of dirty trick was being played on me. Voronin knew that I had just come out of camp. He probably knew that Olga had left. He knew that I drank. Perhaps he wanted to provoke me into some sort of criminal action. But why? What had I ever done to him? I could find no answer. The simplest solution would have been to have a drink and forget it all but I decided not to succumb.

The next day I felt just as bad. It was the third day I had not drunk and nor had I eaten. I went into the kitchen and listened to the noises in the building around me. Then I heard voices on the landing. I stood by the front door with my ear to the crack, but all I could hear was babble, punctuated by whistles and shrieks.

I lay down to read again, but I could not concentrate on my book. The lines danced before my eyes without making sense. I put the book down and lay waiting for nightfall, hoping for sleep to bring relief.

That morning I had thrown my quilt into the stove to warm the room; now the acrid stench of burning cotton wool annoyed me. I wanted to open a window but did not dare after the business with Voronin. I listened to noises outside. The wind had abated and the street now roared with cement mixers driving to the building site down the road.

Suddenly I heard my name from the other side of the wall. I took my metal mug and placed it against the door to listen, as I had learned in prison. Bloody hell, they were discussing how to get me sent to jail!

"It didn't work last night," said Voronin.

"You must do something to get rid of that parasite," I recognised the voice of a woman who lived on the floor above me, "How can I bring up my children decently with him around?"

"His poor wife," said another, "no wonder she left him. Did you see the low-life he brought in last week?"

'Hypocrites!' I thought, 'You bitches are not averse to the bottle yourselves and when you're drinking the whole block has to know about it.'

I thought of jumping out on them but decided this might also be some sort of provocation. If they could accuse me of starting a fight I would go back to camp for sure.

Judging by the noise, everyone in our block was assembled on the landing. Then I heard Voronin address his eldest son: "Dimka, go down into the street and throw stones at the windows. Then there will be material evidence to have Petrov arrested."

I rejoiced. They did not know that I had nailed up the balcony door. But they were many and I was one. I knew the disposition of the police well enough—they did not need proof: once they had their denunciations, everything would proceed as smoothly as a knife through butter.

I turned off the light in order to see what was happening in the street. Dimka was walking about below, his eyes on the ground.

'Hah, he won't find any stones. The snow is too deep,' I thought.

Dimka began gathering compressed lumps of snow thrown up by the cement mixers and throwing them at the windows of the block. Fortunately the lumps disintegrated before they reached the third floor.

I began to shake with fear and indignation. Not wishing to give up without a fight, I burst out onto the landing and pressed the doorbell of my next-door neighbour. I needed a witness to prove my innocence. My neighbour, a Tartar named Piotr Tukhvatullin, opened the door, looked into my eyes and silently ushered me into the kitchen where he poured me a glass of aftershave.

"Drink!" he said, bringing out a chess board and playing with me for the rest of the night. Sunday morning dawned and Piotr took me to the market with him. He spent the whole day buying animal skins from peasants, keeping me beside him and giving me a top-up whenever I started to get nervous. I felt better, but back in the flat that evening the terror returned. In order not to hear the Voronins' conversation I went into the kitchen. Apathy overwhelmed me. Let them do to me what they will, I thought. Then voices began to come through the wall that bordered on the Tukhvatullins. Piotr's wife was cursing him for getting mixed up with me. He defended himself rather half-heartedly.

I began to suspect that something was not right at all. I went into the toilet and pulled the chain over and over again. Despite the noise of the water I could still hear the conversation on the other side of the wall.

'Delirium tremens! The d.ts!' Running into the kitchen I pulled out my emergency supply but it did not help. The Voronins had started to sing. An opera was coming from the other side of the wall. Voronin was singing solo in a bass voice:

"From wall to wall with his mug
he runs and listens . . .

"He hears nothing!" a chorus of his relations replied.

It was music from *Carmen*. I laughed as tears poured down my cheeks. 'Why the hell does it have to be opera?' I wondered. I was an ignoramus where music was concerned. My only visit to the opera had been a reward for washing our bedroom floor in Riga. I blocked my ears but the voices did not stop. 'If I know I'm hallucinating I have not completely lost control over myself,' I reasoned. I had to do something so I dressed and went outside. It was three in the morning. At the approach of a car I broke into a sweat. The sudden bark of a dog made my scalp tingle and tighten in terror, but I pressed on and managed to reach the first aid post on the main road.

I was put in an ambulance and driven to the psychiatric hospital at Komsomolsk. Two nurses escorted me in through the foyer, weaving around male and female patients who were waltzing like somnambulists to the strains of The Blue Danube. I laughed till my stomach hurt.

I was treated by a Doctor Djmil who convinced me that my visions of the last few days had been nothing more than products of my imagination, except for the dancers in the hospital foyer. They had been real and part of the Doctor's attempts to give his patients a sense of normality.

I calmed down, although I craved a drink. After three days I discharged myself, thinking the best thing to do would be to start work as soon as possible. But my empty flat haunted me with reminders of my family. I ran away, seeking out friends who drank.

After two weeks I returned and spent the whole night sweeping up little black devils who had taken over the flat in my absence. There were several hundred of them, about the size of mice, running about the floor thumbing their noses at me and sticking out their tongues. They teased me for imagining my neighbour with a gun. I was not afraid of them for they seemed more mischievous than evil. I took a mop and briskly herded them into the corner so I could crush them all at once. I worked as diligently as a woman mopping up spilled water. The task took all night, for as soon as I had swept the devils into one corner they jumped over the mop and ran squealing across the floor again.

When my strength gave out I sat down on the bed for a cigarette. The devils ran up my trouser legs as far as the knee, tickling me with their tails. Pulling up my trousers I flicked them off onto the floor like insects. Eventually I could bear it no longer and ran from the house. I wandered all night until my legs brought me back to the hospital. Djmil looked into my eyes and ordered me to get undressed. He gave me a massive dose of aminazine and I finally fell asleep.

Half the people in my ward were alcoholic and the rest insane. The alcoholics were treated with Antabuse; however, we knew that all medicines were poisonous, and it was rumoured that Antabuse diminished potency, so everyone tried to avoid swallowing their tablets. We hid them in our cheeks and then spat them out into the toilet.

The first person I met on the ward was Ivan Shirmanov. An habitual patient in the hospital, he showed me around, telling me not to be scared of the lunatics. Like every supposedly normal person I was wary of them, but I discovered they were not frightening people, simply unfortunate. In the course of my life I had met enough people who could have passed for psychiatric patients; some of the hospital's inmates would not have been out of place in the corridors of power.

One of the patients had the apt name of Vodkin. He had been a chauffeur until drink addled his brain so much he forgot the number of the car he drove. In order not to confuse it with another he would leave the starting handle in when he parked it. Vodkin's colleagues used to take the starting handle and put it in another vehicle. Vodkin would then spend hours trying to start the wrong car. Eventually he was sacked and sent to hospital.

The nurses took Vodkin's pyjama bottoms away to prevent him getting out of bed, but occasionally he would pinch someone's dressing gown and wander into the smoking-room where the alkies gathered. His passion was draughts. Despite his imbecility he always won so no one wanted to play with him. The only way to distract him from the board was to ask him to sing. Kicking up his heels in a peasant dance he would roar:

"We spent the night in Samara
With the MVD
They hit us on the neck
We won't tell anybody!"

To encourage him we all joined in with the chorus: *"The storm raged, the lightning flashed . . . "* until an orderly came to take Vodkin away and tie him to his bed.

I would have done anything to escape the horror of the d.t.s, so in the end I agreed to take Antabuse. However, my previous experiences had made me sceptical of the treatment. Dr Djmil lent me some books by famous psychiatrists but these only fed my doubts. "Doctor," I said to him, "I have concluded that Antabuse is an unnecessary element in the cure for alcoholism. It works on the basis of fear rather than physiological fact. People who think they are going to die if they drink on top of Antabuse probably will. It all depends on your state of mind. Antabuse won't work on me anymore as I have stopped believing in its effect."

Djmil listened to my argument attentively, frowned and said, "Vanya, please don't discuss this with the others. Come with me."

He took me through the wards, pointing at drooling imbeciles.

"That is your future if you continue to drink."

Scare tactics did not work with me, nor, it seems, with the doctor himself. Several years later I heard that Djmil had become an alcoholic. After being sacked by the hospital he could be found with his former patients begging outside vodka shops. This was a great pity, as he was a good person and he did not take bribes.

During my stay at the hospital Djmil had told me about his passion for mountain-climbing. Like many members of the provincial intelligentsia, he understood very well the putrid nature of the society in which we lived. He had chosen a hobby that took him temporarily beyond the confines of our human world and into a battle with the elemental forces of nature. I remembered our geography teacher at school and his passion for hiking.

Other members of the intelligentsia went the way of Sedoy and it looked as though I was heading in that direction too, not that I considered myself a member of the intelligentsia. My leg prevented me from hiking or climbing, so I could not follow the path of Djmil and others.

I decided there was nothing more the hospital could do for me and discharged myself. My first priority was to find Olga and Daisy. Although I pestered her every day, Ludmilla steadfastly refused to reveal their whereabouts. One day, however, I saw a letter in her box on the ground floor. Pulling it out, I recognised my wife's handwriting. There was no return address on the back but I managed to decipher the postmark: Estonia.

The next morning I hauled our washing machine

down to the yard by the rubbish bins and sold it to a passing driver. I bought a ticket to Estonia and set off on the 2,000 kilometre journey, fortifying myself on the way with beer.

After three days I alighted from the train at the town of Kivyili, the nearest of the three Estonian mining towns that the atlas had shown. It was five in the morning. I took the first bus to the far side of town to begin my search. I could have gone to the public health centre but I did not want to embarrass Olga if she turned out to be working there. After my drunken journey I looked repulsive.

The weather was warm and I went into the park to take off my sweater. Just inside the gate was a photo display of buildings that had recently been constructed in the town. One of them was of a kindergarten built in an unusual style. I thought it might be the one Daisy attended. I walked around the town and after an hour I found it. It was playtime and I caught sight of Daisy amongst the children. Making sure she could not see me, I waited until the end of the working day when my wife came to pick her up.

When she saw me Olga looked shocked and annoyed. Then she sighed: "I suppose I knew you would find us sooner or later."

I assured her that her sister had not betrayed her and all I wanted to do was have a talk. We bought bread and yoghurt and went into the woods. Our discussion was fruitless. It was obvious to Olga that I had not given up drinking.

"Look, Vanya, let's give it a year. If you can stay on

the wagon for that time we'll come back to you. If not, I am going to divorce you."

"Agreed," I said, "I'll go back to my parents for a while, get myself straightened out."

We both knew we were kidding each other and ourselves. Seeing that my journey had been pointless, I found out the time of the trains and told Olga not to see me off. I had one rouble left in my pocket. I bought an ice cream for Daisy and cigarettes for myself, so that I would not have to be in anyone's debt by begging them. It would not be easy to leave Estonia without a ticket so I planned to hop onto a freight train. I waited at the station till dusk, when I might be able to slip unnoticed into a goods wagon. However, at about ten in the evening, my wife suddenly appeared. She said she had guessed that I had no money and proposed that I come home to rest in her flat for two or three days until she got her pay. Daisy and Olga went off to sleep at a friend's house. Before she left I asked Olga to lock the door from the outside.

The d.ts began again that night. While I still had some control over myself, I looked about for some form of distraction. Like any woman, Olga had no tools in the house, but I found a manicure set and used that to take her iron apart and put it together again, over and over again. All night long the neighbours on the other side of the walls sang abominations about me. This time the tune was from *The Marriage of Figaro:*

"*He mends the iron,'*
he mends the iron,

> he mends the iron,
> the irrrrrron ... he mends!

Then the chorus joined in: "*Bravo, bravo, bravissimo...*"

I found some cotton wool and stuffed up my ears but it did not help. I began running from one room to the other and back again. I took shower after shower, I heated up a large pan of borshch, anything to distract myself from the horrors. Most of all I was afraid of touching the gas cylinder. I imagined that after the explosion everyone would say: "His wife had only just got settled when that drunken swine arrived and blew the whole block to kingdom come."

In the morning Olga arrived to find me bending over the iron with cotton wool sticking out of my ears. She gave me some medicine that enabled me to sleep a little. The following day she saw me off onto the train. Perhaps she wanted to make sure that I left.

As we parted I reassured her that everything would be all right, but in my heart I knew we would never again be able to live together. Olga could not live with her guilt for sending me to prison and I had no right to inflict my drunkenness on her and Daisy. I could not even bear to see them around me: they were a constant reminder and reproach. 'Even if I stop drinking,' I thought, 'I shall always feel guilty before them. No, we have to get used to living apart.'

I was depressed by the thought of losing my daughter. Although I was of little use to her, she had jumped for joy to see her drunken father at the gates of her nursery, and that was no bad thing.

Fifteen minutes into the journey I was drinking in the company of three girls who were looking for a fourth to make up a hand at cards. They were already drunk. It would have been the grossest indecency to pretend that I did not drink, especially as their invitation coincided with my wishes.

I went back to stay at my parents' flat while I decided what to do next.

Dobrinin poured another glass for my mother. It did not take much to make her drunk. "You can give me all the vodka you want," she shrieked, "but I won't keep quiet. I know you've been seeing that bitch again."

Dobrinin smirked and left the flat, leaving the front door open. He returned with the neighbours from across the landing. They stood in the doorway laughing.

"In case you were wondering what all the noise is about, there you are," he pointed to my unhappy mother sprawled on the divan. She snarled and feebly threw a book at them.

This was too much for me. I shooed the neighbours out with my stick. Then I turned to Dobrinin and pushed him violently against a wall. He sank to the floor, winded. I went to bed.

"I'll fetch the police. Why did you take that bastard in?" I heard Dobrinin in the next room.

"Shut up. Leave it to me. I'll sort him out."

In the morning my mother looked at me with hatred: "What the hell did you attack him for?"

"How can you let him laugh at you like that?"

"It's none of your business. Get out!"

I moved into a hostel and started to drink in earnest again with the other men who shared my hostel room. We had no lack of company for we offered warmth and companionship without wives or mothers-in-law threatening to call the police.

I began work in a pesticide factory. My wife's brother was a technician there and he kept her informed of my condition. Hearing that I was drinking again she put pressure on me for alimomy, promising to pay it back if I stopped drinking. 'She's still trying to exert control over me,' I thought bitterly. In any case I had nothing to send her. My pay-packet came with the cost of visits to the sobering-up station already deducted. Then I had to pay off my debts. It was impossible to break out of this vicious cycle. I could not afford to rent a room of my own, but to live in the hostel and not drink was beyond human endurance. In my free time I went to the local library reading room, but then all the same I had to go home and tip someone off my bed.

I finally decided to leave town. I had had an invitation from a former boss, Gantimirov, to go out and work for him at a chemical plant in Chimkent in Kazakhstan. There was nothing to keep me in Chapaevsk. I was tired of that damned hostel, of shop No. 28 and the sobering-up station. I was sick of my companions, too. They would forget me soon enough.

I packed a change of clothes and a supply of cigarettes. My younger brother Sashka gave me a tape recorder and some Vysotsky tapes. Early one morning in the spring of 1968 I left Chapaevsk on a southbound train.

chapter six

I was awoken by a gentle tap on the shoulder. A policeman stood before me. "It is forbidden to sleep in railway stations, Comrade. Kindly sit up." He saluted smartly and walked off.

Checking my head to see whether it had sprouted a crown overnight, I turned to the dosser beside me: "Did you see that? Am I dreaming?"

"Didn't you hear what happened here last year?"

"No."

"Chimkent exploded. It began when the police arrested a lorry driver on his way back from a party. The driver's wife went to fetch his workmates. By the time they reached the station the police had beaten the man to death. They claimed he dropped dead from alcohol poisoning.

"By evening there was no Soviet authority left in Chimkent. The drivers hijacked bulldozers and flattened the police station. Rioters ran through the town, killing any cops who got in their way. Eventually troops were sent in and in a few days the shops filled with scarce goods. As the town calmed down the MVD went around asking questions and people began to disappear. The cops involved with the driver's death were transferred to another area; their chief became head of a prison camp. You can guess the fate of the rioters who were sent there. Komsomol volunteers and troops kept order in town. We had no police force for several months."

I laughed and settled down to sleep again. The next time a cop woke me I told him to book me a hotel room; he left me alone. A lot of people had moved into the station. At night we gathered in the waiting room and listened to Vysotsky; by day we went about our separate business.

I had no luck finding work. Gantimirov was away on a business trip and the plant would not take me on without his approval. I tried other factories. There were a lot of jobs going, but none of them provided accommodation. I looked for a flat but was offered grim cages so far out of town that I refused them.

My money was melting like Tien Shan snow, although I was not drinking and barely eating. In the end I took a train to Tashkent and then jumped another to Fergana, where a cousin of my mother's lived. As everyone knows, the tongue leads to Kiev and I was able to find my relative by asking around. He helped me get a job in a chemical factory and the plant gave me a place in a suburban hostel.

The area of Fergana where I lived was modelled on the Cheryomushki district of Moscow, with rows of five-storey brick blocks, barren shops and dusty roads. Irrigation ditches ran along the streets, but these were choked with dead dogs and condoms. Each year new saplings were planted, only to wither and die in the smog of the huge new chemical plants whose chimneys smoked day and night, covering the Fergana valley with filth. In short, the town was not very different to Chapaevsk.

My work was easy enough, but I sweated and chafed in my protective clothing, rubber boots and gas mask.

In my free time I hung around the hostel growing bored as there was no TV or other entertainment. The lads who shared the hostel never went in to the factory yet they came home in the evenings laden with food and drink.

"Here, Vanya, have some dinner with us," they offered one night.

"No, it's okay, I'm not hungry," I lied.

"Try it, it's dog meat."

"Well, I'll just take some salad." I knew people sometimes ate dog meat as a cure for tuberculosis but I was reluctant to try it. After the lads and I had sealed our acquaintance with a bottle I asked how they managed to live so well.

"We only took a job at the plant to get these rooms and a residence permit. We wouldn't work for the pittance they pay there. Come with us tomorrow and we'll show you how to make some real money."

In the morning we walked down to the railway line. Some men were unloading planks from a goods wagon, throwing them down as carelessly as if they had been shaking matches from a box. Without asking anyone's permission we set about stacking the planks; at one o'clock some Uzbeks arrived to find us leaning against a neat pile. The Uzbeks, who were building a private house, asked us to load the planks onto their cars. When we had finished they paid us and treated us to dinner. I earned more for that day's work than I would have got in a week in the factory.

I decided then to give up regular work and become a tramp. It would be easy enough in Central Asia. If you tried to live rough in European Russia you usually ended up making a camp bunk your bed. In Asia you could doss down under any bush and there was plenty of casual work to be found. I was excited by the prospect of living without the blessings of regular work, bathhouse on Saturday, and political meetings on Tuesdays.

My new friends and I travelled on to Bukhara and Samarkand, picking up work as we went. I made adobe bricks, dug foundations and painted roofs. We spent the nights at chaikhanas, sleeping on low-slung cots that doubled as tables. In the mornings we drank bowls of green tea as we waited for the alcohol shops to open. Despite being Muslims the Uzbeks were fond of alcohol. They also liked to sit in circles smoking hashish.

"Try this, genuine Kashgar marijuana!" someone offered me.

It gave me nothing more than a pain in my temples. It is just as well that I did not take to hashish. Being an alcoholic was enough.

In Bukhara I worked as a stoker in the brick kilns. You had to be very agile to avoid getting burned. The strongest men earned up to 80 roubles a day, an amount which would have taken me nearly a month to earn back in Chapaevsk. The trouble was that no matter how much anyone earned they never saved a kopeck. They drank it all away and I was no exception. I made so much money that I never had to be sober.

After a while the Central Asian climate began to wear me down. My bones ached and I found it hard to sleep. I decided to return to Chapaevsk. The problem was that however much I earned I could never manage to save enough for a ticket home. After finishing a job I had to toast its completion; by the time I sobered up my pockets were empty and I needed money for my hair-of-the-dog.

I decided to look for work in a more remote area away from temptation. I returned to Fergana, went down to the labour exchange and quickly came to an arrangement with a Korean who had a plantation in the mountains. The man took me up on the back of his motorbike, dipping the machine left and right around tortuous hairpin bends. On left-hand curves my stiff right leg stuck up higher than my head. My hands were shaking so much from my hangover that I feared at any moment I would lose my grip and fly off, hurtling down to the valley floor hundreds of metres below. Rising up through clouds that soaked our clothes and faces in moisture, we finally reached the plantation. Onions, garlic, watermelons and rice grew on high terraces through which glacier water flowed. The Korean's entire family, from tiny children to an ancient grandmother, worked from dawn to dusk, yet they needed extra labour to help weed the terraces. State investigators were bribed to keep away.

I was given a few roubles a day, food and packets of 'beggars of the mountain' cigarettes. We worked barefoot in freezing water while our bodies were exposed to the burning mountain sun. Our backs blistered and our hands cracked. At night we climbed into pits lined with paper sacks and threw our exhausted bodies onto heaps of old rags.

The one advantage of working in the mountains was the absence of alcohol. This enabled me to return to Fergana after a month with enough money for a ticket home. Before I could leave town I had to go back to the hostel to pick up my passport. On the way I noticed an inviting bar, with tables laid out under shady trees. 'I deserve a drink to celebrate,' I thought, 'I'll still have plenty of cash for my ticket.'

ALCOHOLICS AND LAYABOUTS! proclaimed our banner in bold white letters on black cloth. We were a filthy procession of swollen-faced men and women. Some had black eyes; some were on crutches. A trolley rolled along behind us, supporting a camera which was filming us for Fergana TV. A local who had had a starring role on a previous march told me that we would appear on the news that night.

We paraded down the middle of the road in full view of shoppers and passers-by. People laughed and shook their heads but no one shouted abuse. They probably thought: 'There but for the grace of God go I.'

The police had picked me up after finding me passed out in a ditch. They hosed me down, put me in a cell for the night and in the morning forced me to stand in the yard with the other detainees while the police superintendent lectured us on the evils of drink. When we returned from the penitential march they made us pay for our night's lodging and each of us was fined 25 roubles, except the two men who had carried the banner; they were excused five roubles of their fines, which no one begrudged them.

After my release I went back to the labour exchange. I was hired by another Korean with a plantation in the mountains, but again on my return I drank away my pay before I could reach the railway station. It was the same story all summer. I took jobs in Kuvasai and Kizil Kiya in Kyrgyzia. Finally, when the weeding season ended, I managed to reach the railway station without being diverted and settled down in the station buffet to wait for the Tashkent train. My disreputable appearance must have given me away for a cop came over and hauled me off. Fortunately some foreigners were staying in Fergana so I did not have to repeat the penitential march.

The police wanted to know why I had not paid my first fine. I was still registered at the chemical plant so I said I was waiting for my wages. The superintendent told a policeman to escort me to my hostel to collect my passport, which they would hold until I paid off my fines. The policeman and I set off on foot. The man was so tired after his night shift that he let me continue alone, making me promise to hand in my passport the next day. That was the last the Fergana police saw of me. I picked up my passport and headed for Margilan.

At Margilan station an Uzbek bought me a ticket and in return I smuggled a caseload of tomatoes to Tashkent for him. I found that city in uproar after a spontaneous explosion of nationalism during a football match between the local Milk Churners team and the visiting Ukrainian Miners. Rioting spread into the streets after the game. The police and local militia broke up fights and then beat up anyone they could find. Train passengers were warned not to walk into the town. I spent a few days in the station trying to find a way home. The conductors on Moscow-bound trains were unusually strict and would not let me on without a ticket. At last a Kuibyshev train pulled in. I approached a young conductor standing on the platform.

"Hey mate, take me along with you."

He looked me up and down and asked: "Have you got any money?"

"Not a kopeck. If I had I would have bought a ticket."

The lad laughed and asked sarcastically: "Would a ride as far as Kuibyshev suit you?"

"It would," I replied, "I shall catch a local train after that."

"So three thousand kilometres isn't far enough for you! Where is your final destination?"

"Chapaevsk," I replied, looking around to see if I might try my luck elsewhere.

"You're from Chapaevsk then?"

"Yes."

"What part?"

"Bersol."

"You're kidding!"

"What would be the point of lying? The train is about to leave and we shall never see each other again."

"Wait," he said, "what street do you live on?"

"Clinic street."

"Do you know anyone on Short Street?"

"Lyokha Pop."

"What about Lyuska Trepalina?"

"Everyone knows her."

Lyuska was the local whore. She used to hang around our hostel. I had only spoken to her a couple of times, but that was enough for the conductor to let me on board.

The train departed and I settled down in a window seat. The endless steppe slid past, as smooth as bone, broken only by a dry shoreline that had once been lapped by the Aral Sea. When we stopped at desolate towns the conductor, whose name was Yura, did a roaring trade selling vodka and cigarettes to crowds on the platform.

"There is no alcohol or tobacco in their shops," he explained. "I have to give a cut to the station master and chief conductor, but I make enough. Have a drink."

The *Sergei Uritskii* was an old man of the Volga, a steamer built in 1912. It stank of dried Caspian roach and the over-ripe melons that were were piled high in baskets on the upper deck blocking everyone's way. It was pleasant to sit on the passenger deck in old wicker chairs under a canvas canopy. Cream silk curtains flapped liked sails through open windows. For two days and nights I gazed at the shoreline, mesmerised by distant cities and hydroelectric power projects.

My friend Oleg from the Astrakhan camp had asked me to come and stay with him. I sold some blood to help the Vietnamese victims of American aggression and bought a ticket. In Astrakhan I found Oleg living in a district built in the popular Cheryomushka style. Although he had an official job checking shop burglar alarms he earned his money in billiard halls. We settled into a routine. I took over his rounds while he went off to play. After lunch I joined him.

Pretending not to know Oleg, I bet on the outcome of the game. With a prearranged signal he let me know how it would end. That way we always won. If he lost I collected money for backing his opponent; if he won our winnings were doubled. No one knew me in the town and we did not broadcast our friendship. All the same we did not win much, just enough to feed ourselves and the family.

Oleg was on the wagon, which was fortunate, as drinking and billiards do not go together. Fights in billiard halls were common and so was cheating. When an apparently stronger player lost there was always a post mortem which rarely ended peacefully. The winner often had to beat up the loser to make him pay. It was forbidden to play for money, so Oleg and I had to be careful. If caught making bets we would have gone straight back to prison.

Life would have been fine had there not been problems on the domestic front. Oleg and his wife Lily were constantly quarrelling. Their punches, slaps and screams would end in no less violent reconciliations. The police had long since stopped responding to neighbours' complaints. They knew that by the time they arrived the combatants would be locked in such a tight embrace it would be impossible to prise them apart. If they managed to arrest Oleg then Lily would turn on them like a tigress. Once, when they tried to arrest Lily, Oleg dangled their daughter out of the window until the police let Lily go.

It was impossible to live in this atmosphere, so after a month I decided to return to Chapaevsk. Before I left, Oleg took me to a village near the sea where we bought 1,000 dried bream for a fantastically low price. In Kuibyshev these fish were in great demand as an accompaniment to beer. I could sell them for enough money to support me for several months.

As luck would have it, the *Sergei Uritskii* was waiting in dock. I just managed to buy a ticket for a place on deck and boarded at the last minute. As I was arranging my bags I heard a familiar voice.

"Vanya! Returning already? Didn't you find your friend?"

It was one of the waitresses, Asya, whom I had got to know on the journey down. She was surprised to see me so soon.

"I did," I replied, "but a husband and wife make one devil. I felt uncomfortable in the middle of their quarrels. I am going home now to sell my fish."

"But you have so many bags and no berth."

I smiled, "I'm alright. I'll sleep under the stars again."

Shyly Asya asked me to share her berth. She was one of those rare women who are untouched by the filth of this world. I could have arrived home not only without the bream but without trousers, money or documents. It would have been as easy for Asya as spitting, but as we bid farewell she would not even exchange addresses. "It is better not to raise hopes," she said. "They are too easily crushed."

I decided not to sell my fish to the thieves and swindlers who ran the market. Instead I gave it to my uncle Volodya in return for an advance. By the end of the week I was back on the bottle again and had forgotten all about the bream. As luck would have it, I bumped into Yura the conductor and was able to thank him properly for the ride.

I moved into a hostel. It was built like pre-war barrack housing except it was made of brick and had an indoor toilet. All day long snotty children played in the corridor under lines of grey underwear. Everyone knew which pair of underpants belonged to whom. If a brassiere fell on the floor you could pick it up, examine it and identify its owner by the way it was patched. Then you'd knock on her door: "Auntie Dusya, here's your bra. The kids were using it as a football."

Domestic rows blew up with boring regularity. Every family drank. The noise only abated in the early morning when the bottles were empty and the shops still closed.

Each morning my hangover got me out of bed as automatically as if I had been going to work. I gathered together bottles from the night before and went next door to shop No. 28, to exchange the empties for a glass of cheap fortified wine. This disgusting brew helped me control myself until ten o'clock when the spirits section opened.

In the morning my hands shook so much that I could not hold a glass without spilling it over myself. If I had a companion with me he would pour the wine down my throat—if not I used a belt; I wrapped one end round the hand that held the glass and passed the other around my neck, pulling on it so the glass reached my lips.

On the days when the shop was out of wine we had to look for eau de Cologne or aftershave lotion. I found these hard to drink on an empty stomach. Furniture polish was the worst—that was real poison and always made me puke. However, once I had lined my stomach with a hair-of-the-dog, I could drink whatever came my way.

Alkies from the whole district congregated in my room. It was warmer than the street. I opened the day's session by banging my fist on the table:

"What's the fucking use of thinking?
Fill your glasses and start drinking!"

Each person took a bite from a stale hunk of bread on the table as they passed the bottle around. When a new face appeared at the door I shouted: "Come in! Welcome to the communist state. Don't worry about a thing. Put on what you like and sleep with who you like. In the morning we sort out clothes and girls."

I tried to avoid my former workmates. They were all drinkers too, but unlike me, they did not comb the shops for lacquer and varnish. When I saw my mother in the streets I ducked out of her sight. Unfortunately ours was a small town and well-wishers had informed her of my descent into street drinking. One day she came down to shop No. 28 and bundled me into a taxi. She had a bag already packed. We drove out to a hospital at Rubezhnoye, a former country estate where Catherine the Great's lover, Count Orlov, had kept thoroughbred horses. After the revolution the house had been converted into a hospital, but 50 years of Soviet power had brought it to a state of collapse.

The director turned a blind eye if patients got drunk on occasions; the most important thing was to repair the place. A condition of treatment was that each patient had to work four hours a day without pay. They painted and plastered walls and built a dacha in the grounds for the director. My job was to watch the hospital's water tank, making sure it never overflowed or ran dry.

"Go on, drink your damned vodka! Drink the filthy stuff!" the doctor stood in the middle of our circle, conducting us like a circus ringmaster. We each had a bucket between our knees. The doctor had injected us with apomorphine before making us drink a warm solution of bicarbonate of soda. Then we drank vodka from the three bottles we each had been told to bring with us to the hospital.

The doctor examined everyone's bucket. I could never manage to throw up, so he made me drink a mixture of vitriol, castor oil and vaseline. The next morning I stuck two fingers down my throat while the doctor's back was turned. Anything was better than drinking that dreaded cocktail again. After a dozen sessions I started to vomit blood and they took me off the treatment—a blood vessel had burst in my stomach.

Next we were treated with Antabuse, with a cruelty and intensity I had not experienced before. After my dose the doctor made me drink 20 grammes of vodka. I began to suffocate. My chest felt as though it was buried under rocks. As I struggled for breath the doctor held up a hand mirror. I saw my face turn purple and then deathly white. My hands and feet were freezing. I was wrapped in blankets and the doctor monitored my blood pressure. Whenever necessary they gave me an oxygen mask. With each treatment they increased the dosage of vodka. When I returned to consciousness, only half alive, the doctor leant over me and said, "There, you see, in hospital, in the presence of a doctor, you almost died. What will happen to you if you have a drink outside? You will die! You'll die gasping like a dog!"

Despite that torture I still did not believe in the efficacy of Antabuse; however, I stayed off the bottle for a few weeks after my release. I hoped to keep sober for long enough to find a more interesting circle of friends.

I was sick of hanging around the vodka shop with completely degraded people. After my two unsuccessful attempts to escape Chapaevsk, I began to suspect that I would only find the company I desired in Moscow. 'In the capital there must be people who live life in the fullest sense of the word,' I thought to myself, 'who write novels and read poems to each other. But how could I live among those parasites? They think they are above us provincials, but all the while they bleed us dry. They live off our backs. They think themselves so superior, yet to boast that one is a Muscovite born and bred is as absurd as boasting that one was born on Saturday.

'Even if I decided to go to the capital I would have to live rough, since I know no one there. And all those plate glass windows reflecting the ugly curve of my leg will be a constant reminder of my disability.'

So I did not go to Moscow; instead I went out to the steppe. My sister's husband Yura kept bees and he needed someone to watch the hives over the summer. The last remnants of the ancient forest that once covered most of Kuibyshev province had been cut down during the Great Patriotic War[1]. Now the steppeland crops were protected from dry winds by strips of plantation. These trees had grown from saplings which my classmates and I had helped to plant twenty five years beforehand.

Along the edge of the plantation were some 80 beehives, belonging to different owners. They took it in turns to bring me food, water, tea and cigarettes. Yura

[1] The Great Patriotic War is the Russian name for the Second World War.

lent me a tent, camp bed and a pair of Wellington boots. He asked if I wanted a dog but I declined. 'She will bark at every wild animal that passes,' I thought.

I quickly became attuned to the life of the forest. After a few days I put my watch away for I learned to tell the time by the sun and the stars. I noticed that the magpie chattered in quick alarm at the approach of a human, while his chatter had a different timbre when an animal was passing. When the ants started to scurry faster, trying to cover the entrance to their nests, I knew it was time to take some dry wood into my tent. Sure enough, leaves would rustle, the mosquitoes would bite more viciously, and then I'd hear the first patter of raindrops on my tent roof.

The birds would not let me sleep through the forest dawn, but that was a blessing. I rose to the nightingale's song, edging out of my tent and sitting absolutely still, not even smoking. The bird took no notice of me and sang on, beautifully and forcefully. 'It is not just singing for love,' I thought, 'for the female is already sitting on her eggs. Where does that power comes from?'

When the nightingale fell silent I set off to look for mushrooms. In my childhood Grandfather Dobrinin had taught me how to search for them; he had even known by the smell of the wood what type of mushrooms grew there. The best time to look for them was on days after rain. I might gather two or three basketfuls of saffron milk caps, orange-cap boletus, russula and agarics. Where there were oaks I might strike lucky and find the prized honey agaric. I gave most of my mushrooms away to the beekeepers when they arrived with my provisions.

Later in the day I went to the steppe to pick bunches of St John's wort, greater celandine and milfoil for my sister, who used them for folk remedies.

Rainy days got me down. It was boring and uncomfortable to sit in the tent for hours on end. I had asked Yura and the others not to bring vodka, but all the same I felt restless. To distract myself from my thoughts I carved pieces of wood into statuettes and twisted plastic telephone wires around bottles. I had learned the technique in prison; with a hook made from a bicycle spoke I formed knots into pictures and designs. When I had finished I gave the bottles to the beekeepers who were happy to take them home to their wives.

Just as I used never to tire of looking at the sea, so I would sit for hours gazing across the blue undulations of the steppe. Sometimes a rare bustard hovered overhead, or a distant herd of boars ran through one of the gullies that scarred the landscape. Seven centuries ago Mongol horsemen had camped on these grasslands, for they did not know how to live in the forest. Sometimes when a lorry raised dust on a far-off road I half-closed my eyes and imagined I saw horsemen of the Golden Horde galloping along the crest of a ridge.

Now I feel nostalgic for those days in the forest; even for rainy days with the sound of drops beating rhythmically on the tent roof and the air full of the sharp scent of herbs hanging up to dry.

When summer ended I packed up my tent regretfully and Yura drove me back into town. Each beekeeper gave me a kilo of honey and a small sum of money. I had nowhere to go except the hostel. My former plant would not take me back because of my poor work record. 'Damn them,' I thought, and exchanged my honey for samogon.

chapter seven

There was nothing but Benedictine on the shelf of shop No. 28.

"Let's buy a bottle," I said.

"Are you crazy?" my mate Tarzan exploded. "That's a women's drink. Let's get some cucumber face lotion from Auntie Dusya."

"But Benedictine's stronger than vodka. I used to drink it in Riga."

"Okay, you win."

Tarzan and I wandered off to the park with our Benedictine. We were on our third bottle when Pashka Plaksin joined us. Pashka was famous in Chapaevsk as an alcoholic and a master sewer of felt boots. Many people made boots on the quiet for it was as absurd to look for them in the shops as it would have been to ask for a ferry boat at a chemist. Pashka's boots were the best in town—to own a pair was like having a Pierre Cardin suit in your wardrobe. Those who wanted to jump the queue would slip him a bottle of something. That is how Pashka became a drunkard. In the mornings he shook so much he could not even pull up a glass with his scarf. Someone had to slip a stick between his lips and pour the wine straight down his gullet.

Pashka produced two bottles of pure surgical spirit donated by a grateful customer. The next thing I knew was an agonising pain in my head and back. I opened my eyes to see someone giving me an injection.

"What did you drink?" a voice asked.

"Surgical spirit," I rasped.

"You can't get that in the chemists. Where did it come from?"

"A friend gave it to me."

"That was no friend. If the police had not found you and brought you here you would have died. That was industrial spirit and it has burned up your kidneys."

It seemed that after leaving Tarzan and Pashka I had fallen into a snowdrift. Some passing police had pulled me out and hauled me in to the sobering-up station. A nurse declared me to be on the point of death, so they called an ambulance. It would have spoiled their records if yet another drunk had died in their charge.

The hospital washed out my kidneys and discharged me. Sober again, I was taken on by a plastics factory, but I soon began to resent the working life. When I was drinking the only problem I faced had been how to get over my hangovers; now I was working like a donkey for nothing in return. I was hardly earning enough to buy bread. Most of my pay went to the sobering-up station where I had been 14 times since returning from the forest. Soon I stopped going to work; it seemed too futile.

Despite my recent brush with death I began drinking again. By now the local police were sick of the sight of me, so the next time they picked me up they gave me a beating and put me on a charge of drunken hooliganism. They waited five days for my black eyes to fade, but even then the judge at my trial asked:

"What happened to your face?"

"A bag of fists fell on my head," I replied.

The judge decided I was capable of responding to treatment and sentenced me to two years in an LTP[1]. It lay about thirty miles away, beside the village of Spiridonovka. Life in the LTP was easier than in other camps, for we were classed as sick men rather than criminals. Our guards were unarmed and letters were not censored.

The village of Spiridonovka was a miserable collection of hovels surrounded by a strict regime camp and the LTP. While the village children played 'prisoners and warders', driving each other in convoys through the mud, their parents worked in the camps. The villagers dedicated themselves to meeting the prisoners' needs, smuggling in vodka, cigarettes and an astronomical amount of tea which they sold for a healthy profit.

Treatment was compulsory but I categorically refused to take Antabuse, despite a promise of remission. Although in the past I had swallowed it voluntarily I would not have it forced down my throat. They sent me to the isolator a few times and then gave up on me.

The doctor in charge of our treatment was a sadist called Bityutskaya. "You will not receive parcels here. You have already caused enough suffering to your families," she announced. It did not make much difference to me as I had no one to visit or send in food. Later many of us painted *In Vino Veritas* on the back of our jackets. When the doctor walked past we turned our backs so she could fully appreciate the effects of her treatment.

---

[1] An LTP was a punitive treatmen centre: basically a labour camp for alcoholics who were also supposed to receive treatment.

As I walked into the barracks with the other newcomers an older man came up and introduced himself: "I'm Vassya-the-thief-alias-Honeycake. I've been through Rome and the Crimea, fire and water, brass trumpets and devil's teeth. I'm the orderly around here, so any of you who fancies a cushy job has to clear it with me first, okay?"

Vassya looked around. Spotting a defeated-looking country lad, he asked, "You there, what's your name?"

"Trofim Ivanich."

"You look like an intelligent chap. Give me a goose and you can guard the stationery store."

Trofim persuaded his wife to smuggle in a goose. She probably felt guilty for having committed him to the LTP. Trofim was delighted to be given such an easy job and went off to perform it conscientiously.

At evening roll call there was one person missing; ten recounts established that the absent man was Trofim.

"Where the hell is he?" asked the guard.

"Working," someone remembered.

"Where?"

"Guarding the shop," replied an innocent newcomer.

"Who told him to do that?"

"An orderly," replied another innocent.

No one could prove anything against Vassya; the goose had already been eaten and Trofim received his first lesson in camp life.

Unlike many inmates Vassya was fond of talking about his past: "I grew up on a farm in the Kuban. When the Nazis arrived in '42 I went to work for them as a groom." He paused. "Don't turn up your noses brothers, I had to eat. They needed me to look after their horses so they took me with them when they retreated. We ended up in Hungary. By then it was obvious to any idiot that the Germans were losing the war. I slipped away and joined up with our boys in Poland.

"After the war I went home to the Kuban and everything would have been fine, if my mother had not had to show off to the women at the well. When her neighbours were boasting of their sons' exploits she produced a picture of me with my chest covered in medals. Someone noticed these were fascist decorations. I had borrowed a regimental dress for the photograph; I could hardly pose with a broom and bucket of horse dung. So I was denounced and given ten years for collaboration.

"Since then I've been in more camps than I can count. The truth is I don't care much for life on the outside, what with residence permits, housing queues and trade union meetings. After a month I'm ready to see the inside of barbed wire again."

Early one morning a huge turd appeared in the snow near the accounts office where officers' wives worked. It was about twelve centimetres in diameter. Beside it lay crumpled newspaper and a pile of dog ends. A group gathered around the monstrosity. It could only have been produced by a giant—yet normal-sized footsteps led to the spot.

Vassya appeared to be more affronted than anyone else. "Citizen lieutenant," he said to the officer who had come to inspect the offending object. "This is disgraceful hooliganism, especially in the presence of women. I propose that everyone's orifice be measured in order to find out who is capable of such an outrage."

I had my own suspicions, for that week I had noticed

Vassya collecting something in a plastic bag which he kept carefully hidden away. Later when the fuss had died down he confessed his deed to a group of confidantes. He said he had learned the trick in a camp at Komi.

In the work zone we made shell timers for a Kuibyshev arms plant. Many zeks threw themselves into the job as a distraction from deadly boredom, but none of them got remission. The only guarantee of early release was membership of the SVP. Some zeks thought, 'Okay, I'll put on the armband, but I won't inform on anyone.' However, it did not work like that, for a zek betrayed his fellow inmates as soon as he donned that armband. In a day or two he would be racing the other SVPs to the guardhouse to sing for a two-rouble bonus. Weakness of character turned people into informers, and once they had crossed that line there was no turning back.

We were a friendly brigade. When someone neared his release date we gave him a hand so that he could save some extra money. Although the work was not heavy we depended on chefir[2] to meet our targets. Tea was smuggled in by civilian workers and by the prisoner who went to the village post office for our mail. Zlodian Spiridonich Kitten was the only prisoner allowed out without a guard. He was an artist who painted pictures of kittens on glass to sell in the village. His kittens were all different, with bows and balls and so on. Since the local shop only sold portraits of Lenin there was a huge demand for his work. Zlodian never returned without loose tea slipped in between the pages of newspapers.

2 Chefir is extremely strong tea.

After I had been in Spiridonovka for a year the authorities finally realised that the fight against chefirists was not only useless but counterproductive. A prisoner high on chefir would work like a robot. No tea meant no production target, so the rule was relaxed and production plans were filled.

My co-chefirist was a drug addict known as VV. More of a dabbler than a hardened addict, VV took any tablet he could lay his hands on. He was particularly fond of teophedrin, a mixture of codeine and ephedrine.

"I was a good Komsomolist before I did my military service, but the army changed that. It was not so much the bullying that got me down, though that was bad enough. No, it was being surrounded by so many fools who felt important for the first time in their lives. Now I spit on everything.

"It was my mother who sent me here. She did not like the company I fell into after I left the army. It was not what she had in mind for her only son."

VV and I shared our tobacco and vodka, most of which came into the camp in hot-water bottles thrown over the fence. Almost everyone who was freed from the LTP remembered his mates this way.

One of my fellow prisoners was named Kim, although he was not Korean. His name was an acronym for Communist International Youth. The son of ardent Bolsheviks, Kim was known throughout Chapaevsk as an inveterate drunkard. Kim spent hours on his bunk, dreaming with his chin resting on his drawn-up knees. Suddenly one evening he cried aloud, "Okay! The first thing I do when I get out will be to buy a rusty bike."

"Why a rusty one?" asked his neighbours.

"So no fucker will steal it!" Kim waved a nicotine-stained finger in the air.

"But what do you need a bicycle for, Kim? To ride to the Gypsies for vodka?"

"No, I've had enough of vodka! I'm going to take up fishing. Just think how peaceful it will be to sit on the river bank beside a bonfire, with silence all around and no police, trade unions or Party bosses. Like a fairy tale!"

"And what are you going to do with the fish, Kim?"

"What do you mean? Eat them of course."

"But supposing you don't manage to eat them all up? You are so thin, a few fish would make you burst!"

"If there are any left over I'll sell them."

"And what will you do with the money?"

"Money?" Kim thought for a minute. "Just shut the fuck up you bastards! You don't even let a fellow dream!"

A few weeks after his release Kim was brought back in, shaking and hungover.

"Where's your bike?" we asked.

"I'm like a bike myself," snarled Kim, "a bike falls over when no one rides it and I peg out if I don't have a drink."

After a month Kim started again. "Okay, enough! I'll buy a bike when I get out!"

I grew tired of dormitory conversation about who had drunk how much and who had slept with whom. To relieve the boredom I devised a joke. I wrote a letter purporting to be from 'Sima', the wife of 'Fedya'. When letters were given out all the Fyodors in the barrack came forward but none recognised the handwriting.

There was no return address on the envelope. Then by collective decision the letter was opened and read aloud. It could have been written to any one of us: *Divisional Inspector Paramon often drops by* . . . this was interrupted by a roar of knowing laughter . . . *At last I have dried out the mattress* . . . the reader continued as 300 voices jeered at the unknown Fedya for wetting his bed . . . *I salted the cucumbers and yesterday in the herring queue Paramon's wife Agafya slapped my face* . . . "

In the morning all the Fedyas in the camp came forward to prove their wives were not called Sima. One of them, who happened to be married to a Serafima, brought a collection of letters to show that her handwriting was not that of 'Sima'. After a week another letter arrived from Sima. The contents revealed that she had had a reply from her Fedya. The whole zone set out to uncover the mysterious man. Only after a third or fourth letter did people start to guess that I was the author. Then they clamoured for more: "We want something to cheer us up after work."

That year there was a wave of prison riots all over the country. Discontent also grew in our camp. A new Godfather arrived and he began a campaign of intimidation. Our letters were torn open before they reached us and visitors were roughly searched, especially women. A prisoner from the neighbouring criminal zone went on the run and this was used as an excuse to torment us with endless counts and recounts. One evening a guard walked through our barrack with an alsatian on a slackened chain. It lunged at us, snarling and dribbling saliva. A couple of men who protested were taken out to the punishment cells.

'They say you can divide people between cat lovers and dog lovers,' I thought, 'but I would add a third category: alsatian lovers. We can't put up with this treatment for much longer.'

That night we gathered to discuss what to do. Someone suggested writing a letter to Brezhnev; another said we should kill a dog. Suddenly, to my own surprise, I leaped onto a bunk and shouted at them: "Tossers! Cowards! All this talk is useless!"

The protestors turned to me; some tried to knock me down off the bunk. Others asked, "Well, what do you suggest then?"

"A strike! We stay in bed tomorrow and refuse to go to work until our demands are read by higher authorities. We will write a list of complaints and smuggle a copy out to the newspapers. If the authorities refuse to give way we'll go on hunger strike."

"Idealist!" muttered an older prisoner, but most of the men agreed to my proposal. We chose a committee of four volunteers and I wrote out a list of complaints.

The next morning no one left their bunks except the cook and the man who stoked the boiler. Not everyone was happy to strike, especially those nearing the end of their sentences, but they didn't want to oppose the collective will. The head of the camp, Major Soldatov, came stomping through the barrack, at first abusing us and then trying persuasion. Four men handed him our list of demands and he went off to phone his superiors.

After a week an MVD commission arrived. To our amazement, half our demands were met. Weapons were removed from the zone, we were allowed to wear sweaters and warm underwear, the food improved, visitors' rooms were enlarged, they promised to put a TV in the rec room and to supply any books we requested. I immediately compiled a list and they brought in all the books I had ordered, even ones that were forbidden on the outside such as Schiller-Mikhailov's 'History of the Anabaptists'. I expect they could afford to be generous because their libraries were overflowing with confiscated books.

Despite these concessions, the Godfather continued to censor our letters. My friends and I started to write to ourselves, posting letters via different channels. We covered the pages with meaningless words, sprinkled with numbers and symbols. Let him waste his time trying to decipher these, we laughed.

Thanks to the barrack stoolies the Godfather knew the strike had been my idea. He had his revenge one day when VV and I got completely pissed at work. One of our freed companions had thrown a bottle over the fence. Medvedev, the head of the work brigade, drove us back to the barracks saying we would face the music in the morning. The Godfather ran in to see us, accusing us of making trouble while drunk.

"Phoo, phoo, phoo, get out, get out," we rushed at him, flapping our arms and puffing vodka breath in his face.

He had not brought an escort, so he left, muttering threats. We did not care, for we were waiting to be dealt with by Medvedev, who ranked higher than the Godfather. After a few minutes guards came and hauled us off to the isolator.

In the morning the Godfather raged at us: "You will be punished under article 77 for interfering with an officer in the line of his duty and causing mass disorder."

This charge was considered worse than murder and punishable by anything from eight years to execution by firing squad. We refused to answer the Godfather's questions or admit to anything. "Bring Major Soldatov to the isolator. We won't say anything until he is present."

The Godfather laughed in our faces. "I can assure you that Soldatov will not come."

"But he must. He is head of the camp."

"He won't."

On hearing this we began a hunger strike. A few days later we were taken in a Black Maria to Kuibyshev jail. Our strike had been in vain, because Soldatov was on holiday that week.

Kuibyshev jail was full of men who had taken part in a riot that made ours look like a children's tea party. I heard about it from a prisoner in my cell: "It began when a packet of tea was thrown in and landed on the strip of ploughed earth between the inner and outer wires. As a prisoner stretched his hand through to recover the tea a guard shot him in the leg. Zeks nearby threw stones at the soldier, who fired a few shots in return. News spread around the zone. When the SVPs got wind of a revolt they ran off to the guard house. A couple of them who didn't make it were beaten to death.

"We broke into a workshop and found a tank of diesel fuel. We soaked our jackets in the oil, lit them and threw them through the windows of the guards barracks. The zone was set on fire. As the clubhouse burned down someone pulled out the piano and played as we destroyed the rest of the zone. Some prisoners armed themselves with iron bars and took over the isolators, killing a guard in the process. That day we were possessed by a sort of demonic joy.

"The camp director tried to stop us. I have to admit he was a brave man, for he came out without an escort. He seemed to be prepared to listen so we started to tell him our grievances. Then a zek lost his patience and hurled a waste bin at the director's head. Rage took over again and the director was severely beaten; he died later.

"No one touched the nurses in the camp hospital. One of the zeks with authority led them across to the guard room. The cruel thing is, I've just heard he got eight years; they said that if he had the authority to protect the women he might have intervened to end the riot.

"Troop carriers surrounded the zone and a helicopter circled overhead. A voice played over loudspeakers: 'Citizen prisoners! Cease this mass disorder immediately!' We began to wonder why the soldiers did not storm the place to restore order. It seems they were waiting for orders from Moscow.

"When the day ended we realised we had nowhere to sleep and nothing to eat. We threw stones at anyone who tried to enter the zone, but the night was cold and by the next morning we had lost our enthusiasm. They came for us in Black Marias and we no longer had the energy to defend ourselves.

"We were sent to different jails in the region. I was taken to Syzran, where I opened my big mouth. Some bastard of an SVP overheard me and here I am, looking at another five years. I did not kill anyone or beat any guards. What a mess. If I hadn't got mixed up in that business I would be out next year."

This man's story depressed me, for I too was looking at a longer sentence, and this time it would be in a camp rather than a 'treatment centre'. After a few weeks VV and I came up for trial. Fortunately for us the Godfather could not produce a witness. When we had thrown him out of the barrack there had been only one other man present, and he had been in a state of Antabuse-induced psychosis. This man, Suvaikin, suffered from a form of schizophrenia. When the Godfather came into our barrack for us Suvaikin had cowered in a corner pointing a piece of plywood at him, shouting, "Bang! Bang!" Our charge was reduced to hooliganism. Even so, we got four years each.

Four years! I tormented myself trying to imagine such an endless length of time. But my cellmates congratulated me. Well done! That's nothing! It was true that many people got longer sentences for lesser crimes, but sometimes I felt that I was losing my mind.

Then the impossible happened. Our sentences were reduced to one year thanks to VV's mother. As director of a Syzran department store, she was an important person and able to hire a good lawyer. He won our case at the court of appeal. A year of my original sentence had already passed, so another did not make any difference. I would simply serve out my term in a different prison. VV and I were moved to Barkovka near Toliatti.

The camp at Barkovka was strict regime, full of SVPs and headed by a bastard called Dubov. It lay near an industrial dump which burned continually, covering the area in a black cloud. When the wind blew in our direction it was impossible to breathe without choking on the stench of burning plastic.

The industrial zone was a brick-making plant separated from the living area by a high fence with gates and watch towers. Three times a day a new shift went through the gate; the factory worked around the clock. There were two brigades in each shift; one took the heavy wet bricks from wagons and loaded them into the kilns, the other pulled the scorching bricks out of the kilns. Although gloves were given out once a week, they wore out before one shift was over. Zeks wound old cloths around their hand but these did not protect them from serious burns. Quotas were never met and more than half the bricks were scrapped, which meant no pay bonus and no early release. The equipment was old and the kilns were always breaking down; when this happened blame fell on the inmates.

Barely a week passed without a zek inflicting an injury on himself to get out of work. He would wrap a jacket around his arm and rest his elbow and wrist on two bricks, while another worker smashed a piece of wood down on his arm. The administration did not hasten to bring medical assistance even when the injury was accidental. One man had the courage to break his leg; it healed badly, leaving him an invalid for the rest of his life.

In the morning we were woken by the scrape of metal keys on bunk posts and driven out for morning exercises. Apart from a few enthusiasts, most of us just shuffled about on the spot, taking surreptitious puffs on cigarettes hidden in our fists and cursing the cold wind that gave us goose pimples. Then we were driven to the dining room to drink rotten fish soup at greasy, slimy tables. At eight o'clock we formed work detachments and were sent out to the kilns or workshops.

Plenty of spirit was brought into the work zone by civilians, for it was impossible to search everyone; the problem was when to drink it, for the place was crawling with SVPs who would have reported anyone who got drunk at work. It was also almost impossible to carry the bottles back at the end of a shift. The prisoners surmounted this difficulty by pouring the spirit into condoms and putting these inside safety fuses taken from the kilns. Then they threw the fuses over the fence into the living zone. Dogs ran over the ploughed earth between the fences but they were quite stupid. They ran up barking when prisoners shouted, 'water!', only to have hot water poured on their noses. After that the animals stayed away when they heard the cry. When the zeks were ready to throw the fuses over one of their mates would start a fight to distract the guards. Most of us had played skittles at some time in our lives so we could throw far and accurately.

My crippled leg saved me from the kilns. Instead I was sent to make fluorescent lamps in a separate workshop. There I made friends with a man who had deliberately broken his arm. Sanka Murzaev was a Tartar from Chapaevsk. My wife had attended his mother during her numerous pregnancies. She gave birth so often that during the rare times she was not pregnant her empty belly flapped down like an apron.

Sanka had had a series of different 'fathers' and eventually ended up in a children's prison where he became very fastidious. He would never pick up bread or dog ends from the ground, he would not share a table with a loud or messy eater and he made his bed as neatly as a soldier does. When I got to know him his arm was healing and they were threatening to send him back to work in the kilns. Workers who broke their arms usually only got a couple of months off. Sanka had plenty of peasant cunning and managed to outwit them by writing a letter to a friend, detailing escape plans. He tried to pass it out via a zek suspected of being a stoolie. The plan worked like magic and the letter fell into the Godfather's hands. Sanka was categorised as a potential escapee and banned from the workzone.

Another lad who worked with us was so stunted he could have passed for a twelve year old child. His prison jacket reached to his toes. "That's our Pakhan[3]," said Sanka. "Poor little sod. I knew him back in children's camp. His mother was a prostitute. He's never known home cooking or sweet pies, but he's been sucking on vodka since he was a toddler. His mother used to send him out in the mornings to pick up dog-ends from the streets. Then he had to fend for himself while she entertained her clients. He survived by snatching bread from people's hands, running off and eating it in entranceways. After his mother died of TB Pakhan took to the streets. He was soon arrested for theft and sent to a children's prison. I got to know him there. I felt sorry for him as he was always being beaten

---

[3] In criminal jargon a Pakhan was a leader of a gang of thieves. Usually he was a retired thief who sent younger lads out to work for him, a sort of Fagin character.

up. Once they stuffed him in a locker and threw him out of a first floor window. Now he's blind in one eye and he can't hear much. One day he stabbed one of his bullies to death. He got six years."

Instead of becoming feral and cruel as a result of his treatment, Pakhan was sullen and withdrawn. He reacted to simple acts of kindness with great suspicion. Once I had met my quota I helped him finish his, and then we got down to the important business of preparing 'Boris Fyodorovich' (BF glue). Pakhan stuck close by my side, for unlike the others I did not tease him.

"Pakhan, over here," I called, adding water to BF glue and pouring it through a filter. On some days I collected as much as two litres of spirits. It was risky to store the alcohol so we drank it straight away. There were more than enough volunteers. When he had drunk his fill of BF Pakhan would hide under the workbench and go to sleep wrapped in his jacket.

When Pakhan was nearing his release date a Toliatti factory sent someone to offer him a job. The emissary was a young Komsomol girl who had brought him some clothes—several sizes too large for him. He stood sullenly before her in his enormous jacket, the lining bulging through rips in an imitation of a medieval courtier. Courteously, the girl asked, "Are you thinking of taking a correspondence course when you get out of here?"

Too deaf to hear her question, Pakhan cowered in a corner, shouting, "It wasn't me! I didn't fucking do it!"

Pakhan was reluctant to leave our company. On the day he was due to be released, he ran off and hid. We eventually found him huddled under a workshop bench, his thin childish hand gripping a jar of BF.

Pakhan looked up at me and smiled his toothless grin: "Vanya, wouldn't it be fucking wonderful if we could feel like this all the time?"

chapter eight

Everyone leaving camp planned to find a good job, marry, get ahead, and of course, never end up inside again. I did not suffer from these illusions, but nevertheless I was worried about what I would do after my release. I had nowhere to live in Chapaevsk and my former plant was refusing to take me back. To apply anywhere else with a passport like mine[1] was not a cheerful prospect. Some of the lads who were up for release asked me to come and live with them, but it was evident how that would end up. I dreamed of a life as a lighthouse keeper or a watchman at an observatory. I wanted to go somewhere far away from so-called civilization, deep in the taiga where there were no Party organizations or vodka shops. Remembering how peaceful I had felt in the forest looking after Yura's bees, I decided to seek out a similar kind of existence, far away from Chapaevsk.

"I am never going back to work," I announced to Sanka and VV. "I've inhaled enough chlorine and buried too many workmates. It's a pointless life. Everyone says they'll do their ten[2] years and then get out,

---

[1] Prison records were written in internal passports which had to be shown when applying for a job or a place to live.
[2] After ten years in a hazardous job a worker was entitled to early retirement.

but by then another kid has arrived or they need money to buy a TV set. I am not going down that road. I am sick of being told how to live."

"And how exactly are you going to make your protest? As soon as you open your mouth you'll go straight back inside," VV pointed out.

"Well, if I don't protest openly at least I won't lift a finger to help the system. Anyway, it's only a matter of time before I start to drink again and that'll lead me straight back to the LTP. I'm going south to pick up casual work. In the countryside I'll be free to do more or less as I like. Country people stick more closely to the old ways."

VV turned to Sanka: "So Vanya is going to become a Wanderer[3]. Perhaps you think our beloved Comrade Brezhnev is the Antichrist?"

"The very same."

"And our Founder and Teacher, Comrade Lenin?"

"The Father of Lies."

"The Communist Party of the USSR?"

"The vessel of Satan."

"And all who submit to its authority?"

"Devil's spawn!"

"But this is not the nineteenth century," VV pointed out. "Our Russian people do not support vagabonds and holy fools with the generosity of bygone years. How are you going to live?"

---

[3] A Christian sect that had its roots in Chtherine the Great's reign. It's followers refused to cooperate in any way with the civil and ecclesiastical authorities. They led a nomadic life in the forests of Russia.

"I'll register with a collective farm. No one expects you to work there. The farm will give me a bed and food and my time will be my own. Whenever I get sick of it I can take to the road; if the police pick me up my papers will say I'm a collective farm worker. Vassya-Honeycake told me there are plenty of farms in the Kuban eager to take people on."

VV burst out laughing: "All over the USSR peasants are busting a gut trying to leave the farm. You only find old women, drunks and mental defectives there now, and you want *to* run away to a collective farm!"

"There is nothing left for me here. I no longer have a family. These days I am responsible to no one."

"But you can't run away from yourself," said VV.

"I'm not trying to. All I want to do is get away from everyone who knows me. Especially my mother."

I had sworn never to return home. While I was inside I had heard that my younger brother Sashka had died after drinking tainted samogon on New Year's Eve. He had come home and fallen into a coma in front of my mother and stepfather who were both too drunk to notice their son's condition. By the time they sobered up it was too late to call an ambulance. Perhaps no hospital could have saved him; all the same I blamed my parents for Sashka's death.

VV and I were released together. We had got on well in jail but on the outside our differences began to show. No doubt his important mother would find him some easy work—and no doubt he would soon start taking pills again. Still, he lent me money for a ticket to Sochi.

Before I left Toliatti I went back to Barkovka to meet Sanka on his release day. I knew no one else would come for him so I brought a coat and some clothing to spare him the shame of going home in a prison jacket. Sanka's family lived not far from the hostel where I was staying. He asked me in to meet them.

A mountainous woman opened the door. Fat rolled from her neck to her knees and I saw she was heavily pregnant. Her piggy eyes squinted hard at us for a minute and then she threw her arms around Sanka: "Tolik! You're home. Oi! Grish . . . get a bottle, our lad's back."

Inside the flat youths and girls in various states of drunkeness were draped over chairs and boxes. A few of them turned indifferently to stare at us. Sanka's mother waddled up to a comatose man and punched his head with her huge fist. "Grish, I said wake up you fucking prick-for-legs. Our Misha's back. Give him a drink."

I felt that Sanka would not enjoy the taste of freedom for long.

I took a train to Sochi, and spent a few weeks wandering along the coast of the Black Sea, picking up odd jobs. I fell in with other tramps who helped me to find places to sleep. We preferred the warmth and companionship of railway stations but the police came round continually waking us up. Sometimes we slept on stationary trains in sidings, but local youths barged through the carriages, taking money off those too drunk to resist.

An older tramp showed me how to make some money by standing in the ticket queue for the Sochi hydrofoil and selling my place to latecomers. This man thought I was really wet behind the ears, although I had been a Decembrist and a zek. "How can you reach the age of 35 and not know what a spets[4] is? They have them in all big cities and railway stations. If you get picked up without documents they throw you in for 30 days while they cook up something really incriminating against you. Three times in the spets earns you a year in camp."

I nearly fell victim to this law in the town of Tuapse. A policeman looked at my passport, decided he did not like the look of my face and tore up the document under my nose. Then he arrested me for being without a passport. At the police station I tried to explain what their colleague had done. They laughed and slapped my face a few times. Fortunately, they were too lazy to do the necessary paperwork to give me 30 days. Probably they had exceeded their quota of tramps in jail that month.

I had 24 hours to leave town. From Tuapse I boarded the steamer *Admiral Nakhimov* and sat in the buffet completely indifferent to whether it was taking me north or south. It docked at Novorossisk, where I earned a few roubles by carrying boxes of flowers from the pier to taxis. Having money in my pocket at the beginning of the day bought me a breakfast of beer fortified with essence of dandelion. At night I slept among the feet of giant sailors hurling grenades and charging fascists with bayonets. 'This might be a Hero City,' I thought, 'but their monuments are very draughty.'

The town of Novorossisk was the most important oil terminus in the USSR. Vessels from all over the world docked there. I stuck to the local port, as I knew the

[4] Spets: spetsialnii priyomnik: a lock-up for petty criminals

foreign quays were crawling with plain-clothes police. All the same, my appearance must have betrayed me for one day a young lad approached me at a beer stall, saying he had some business to discuss. Something about him made me suspicious. Before I had a chance to walk away a police car pulled up and I was taken to the spets.

The spets was a row of cells in the courtyard of the town police station. Eight to ten men were crammed into each stuffy cell. We spent our days playing checkers with bread counters and brewing chefir. A skilled chefirist needed only four sheets of newspaper to brew a litre. We had to keep the smoke to a minimum in order not to give ourselves away.

Amongst the guards were a pair of Adegei twins who were much more human than the rest. They gave me some cardboard with which I made chess pieces. One of them suggested a game, but he played badly and I won with ease. One of my cell mates whispered, "Idiot —maybe you should try to lose."

And so I did. It put the Adegei in such a good mood he later threw two loaves of bread into the cell. The next day he gave me a mugful of samogon.

That afternoon my chess game was interrupted by shrieks outside. I stuck my head out of the ventilation hole in our cell door and saw the police bringing five girls into the courtyard. One of them, a tall girl with a shaven head, was wriggling between the Adegei twins and trying to pinch their cheeks. They ducked their heads in embarrassment. A camera stood ready in the yard. The bald girl sauntered over and stood in front of it, striking exaggeratedly glamorous poses.

"Hey, you bastards, get a fucking move on, it's cold out here!" she shouted.

"Come on, Vera, stop pissing about," said the police photographer.

"And what are you staring at?" she suddenly caught sight of me.

I pulled my head in quickly as my cellmates laughed. It hurt me to hear obscenities fall from the lips of such a young and pretty girl.

The girls had been arrested for picking up foreign sailors. The police threatened to tell their workplaces and schools of their 'crimes.' Those who showed fear were blackmailed by the police for sexual favours; those who could not produce documents were put in the women's cell next to ours. It was never empty.

As soon as one of us stuck his head out of the ventilation hole a head would appear from the women's cell. We shouted over to each other and passed food and cigarettes across by bribing the guards. Usually the girls had more to give than we poor tramps had.

From time to time a fight blew up in the womens' cell. They needed to relieve their tension somehow. Vera could not exist for one minute without trying to start a fight. Perhaps having her head shaved had traumatised her. They said it was to get rid of lice, but it was harder for bald girls to work. Clients were suspicious of their state of health.

I savoured my daily exercise in the courtyard; it restored my spirits to look at the sky, hear the noises of the town and feel the rain on my face. One day an elderly man fell into step beside me. He introduced himself as Uncle Misha the Railwayman.

"It's my first time in the spets. It was my own bloody fault for getting drunk and going to the end of the line. In all my 60 years I have never made that mistake. They defrocked me—took away my cap and hammer."

Uncle Misha was a robber who worked the railway lines. "I began my career in the 1920s, after my parents died in the civil war," he said. "I soon learned that stations are the best places for stealing, as people are tightly packed together in unfamiliar surroundings. I got caught a few times but no one handed me in. People preferred to whack me themselves and leave the authorities out of it. I guess they had their reasons.

"Then I learned how to rob goods wagons. I climbed onto their roofs and let myself down inside. I would pick what I wanted, jump off the train and sell my booty to a fence. The only tricky parts were keeping an eye out for the guards and jumping off the moving trains. You had to be fit for that.

"When I got older I found a job on the railways. It did not last long, but I kept my cap and hammer, the tools of my trade. Since then trains have been my only home. I know every station in the USSR down to the smallest country halt. When I get off at a station the first thing I do is study the timetable. I learn them off by heart, both summer and winter versions. They are my daily bread."

I laughed. "You remind me of George Peters, a man I read about in a book. He avoided the police thanks to his excellent knowledge of train times."

Uncle Misha opened his toothless mouth in disbelief: "Did you really read that?"

"Yes, it's in a book by an American writer, O'Henry."

Uncle Misha whistled: "Whew! I always thought that you could never learn anything from books. Everything in them I already shat out the day before yesterday!"

He was silent for a minute before continuing: "Sometimes I notice a lonely-looking suitcase. Then I wait for everyone to fall asleep. It drives me mad when some bloody intellectual takes out a book and reads and reads. You can't tear him away. It would be like trying to snatch a baby from a teat. But it also works the other way. A man might bury himself in the book so deeply you could fuck him up the arse and he'd never notice. So there is a use for books all the same.

"When everyone's asleep I start my technical business. I grab the case, jump from the train, hide alongside it and wait for the next express. Two or three minutes before its departure I push the suitcase into an axle box with my long hammer and then climb inside a carriage. I sit in any empty place, wearing my railway cap so the conductor won't ask to see my ticket.

"When he's passed by I start to tell the other passengers stories that have I picked up on my travels. They're always willing to share their food in return for the entertainment. When I've eaten my fill and slept a bit I get out at a suitable stop.

In any new town the first thing I do is memorise the timetable. Then I go to the nearest beer shop for a few drinks. After that I collect empty vodka bottles—only the cleanest ones. I take them to some quiet wasteland on the edge of town and fill them with water, closing the caps with the help of my bootlaces. Then I return to the station. Late in the evening I take a slow stroll along the platform with a bottle in my hand. I almost always strike lucky. My bottle reminds passengers of their thirst so they call out: 'Oi, mate! Where can I get one?'

"'Not far from here, not far at all. About half a kilometre,' I reply. To them the shop might as well be on the moon.

"The greedy wretches beg me to sell the bottle. I hum and haw until the train is about to depart and then I give in, brushing aside their tips for the service. As soon as the train starts I hop on one going in the opposite direction."

Uncle Misha also bought Asmatol from the chemists. It cost 15 kopecks and was sold as a relief for asthma. If you brewed it like tea and drank it you got completely stoned. It was as effective as a boxful of Noxiron. In Spiridonovka I had watched a prisoner try to climb the fence after drinking Asmatol. The barbed wire ripped his flesh off until it hung in bloody shreds but he seemed to feel no pain. He kept on clawing at the wire until he passed out and toppled to the ground.

"I buy a couple of bottles of wine and mix Asmatol into one of them," continued Uncle Misha. "The wine masks the smell. I select my victim carefully, talking to him for a long time before offering to split a bottle. I have to make sure he will be worth the investment. First we drink the unadulterated bottle of wine until there is only a glassful left in the bottle. I pour this for myself and open the other bottle to pour a glass for my friend. As he drinks it I watch him like a boa constrictor until his eyes unfocus. After that I help myself."

That night I lay awake listening to Uncle Misha snoring beside me. He revolted me. 'How can he take advantage of people's trust and their simple desire to drink?' I wondered. 'Still,' I reasoned, after thinking about it for a long time, 'his crimes are nothing new. People cherry-picked like this even before the revolution. Lot's daughter used this means to become pregnant by her father. In spirit Uncle Misha is no greater criminal.'

The June dawn broke at 4 am. I awoke to find I had run out of matches so I went to get a light from the joggers who were already pounding the sand. To my annoyance everyone turned out to be a non-smoker.

"Damn sportsmen!" I cursed. Then I noticed an ugly, squint-eyed fellow studying me.

"Got a light, mate?" I asked, "I've been looking for one for an hour."

"I don't smoke," he said, but added, "I drink, though."

He picked his jacket off the ground to reveal a bottle of cognac.

"A man after my own heart!" I cried. "Wait five minutes while I get a light. I want a smoke so badly even my arse is dizzy!"

"Go ahead. I'll be here!" he said, pulling his jacket back over the bottle. When I returned we silently passed the bottle back and forth between us, each trying to take smaller and smaller mouthfuls. It was early morning and the shops would not be open for a long time. We introduced ourselves.

"I'm from Kuibyshev."

"And I'm from Tambov," he said, despite his plastic cap proclaiming: I am from Sochi!

"Could you be the Tambov Wolf?" I asked.

"I could be," he replied, "and what is your name?"

"Hadji Nasredeen[5]."

Tambov Wolf laughed: "Oh, Hadji Nasredeen, why do you wear such a high collar on your jacket?"

"To protect my neck from the sun," I replied.

"And if the sun is shining in your face?"

"I turn around and walk in the other direction."

Then I asked, "Where did you get the cognac?"

"Ask me something simpler," replied Tambov Wolf. Then he pulled a three kopeck piece out of his pocket and said, as though pronouncing Newton's fourth law of physics:

"One coin does not clink."

"And two do not make the right sound," said I, producing another coin from my pocket.

"Another eight and we will be OK," he said. I pulled all the small change out of my pocket, but he took only two kopecks from me.

"But you said eight," I pointed out.

"Quite right. Two kopecks and six o'clock in the morning make eight."

The shops opened at six. The sun had risen above the horizon so we had only to wait a while longer. However, alcohol was not sold before 11 o'clock. The battle against alcoholism was in full swing and the masses had to be prevented from getting tanked up before work.

At six Tambov Wolf joined the crowd of grand-

---

[5] Tales of a legendary character called Hadji Nasredeen are part of the folk wisdom of Turkic speaking peoples. In this case Ivan is telling the Tambov Wolf that he is a character who wanders at will.

mothers by the shop doors. After a few minutes he emerged and disappeared behind the monument to drowned fishermen, signalling for me to follow. We sat down on the nearest bench. From his pocket Tambov Wolf pulled out the sister of the bottle we had split earlier and a quarter of a loaf of bread.

"For breakfast," he said. "Don't argue, the bread was come by honestly. The bottle I picked up in passing, to give us something to wash it down with."

Taking advantage of the crush in the shop, Tambov Wolf had darted behind a curtain, pulled out the bottle and tucked it into his belt.

"I wouldn't be able to do that," I said.

"You don't need to. We have enough."

When I became a tramp I had made a pledge that I would never steal or get into a fight. That would keep me out of jail, leaving me free to wander until I grew tired of the life. I soon realised that was naive. Christ himself could not have wandered the USSR unmolested. His attitude of 'take therefore no thought for the morrow' would have got him a year at least, so there was not much hope for the rest of us poor sinners. And sinners we certainly were. We all smoked and cursed and most of us drank.

Later Tambov Wolf went off to steal another bottle, this time from a different shop. We drank it, fell asleep on the beach, and the next day he was gone.

"Vanya! Got a ciggie, darling?" The prostitute Vera was sitting on a bench sporting a black eye.

As it happened I had. Vera was in an unusually calm mood. As we sat smoking companionably she suddenly said, "I was a trainee draughtsman before the Komsomol got hold of me. Some activists picked me up by the beach, saying my button-through dress meant I was a prostitute. They hauled me in and sentenced me as a Decembrist. I had to clean the bogs in the station. When my fifteen days were up I decided I might as well practise what they thought I did anyway. I certainly make a lot more money this way."

She finished her cigarette. "I'll be off to work now. Thanks for the smoke, love. You tramps are okay."

"Well you won't find any moralists among us."

It was time I found a place on a farm. I went down to the town's labour exchange and was directed to a collective farm about 20 kilometres out of town. I set off in the hot sun and hitched a ride part of the way in a truck. However it turned out that the farm administration did not want to take anyone on. I was annoyed at the waste of time. I had not had a hair-of-the-dog and my hands were beginning to shake. Not knowing what to do next, I came out of the office and looked around. There was a lad standing a little way off. Judging by his appearance he was some sort of tramp like me. He ambled over to where I stood.

"Brother, do you know what time it is?" I asked.

"Five to whatever the fuck you like. Are you late for work?"

"Work is not a wolf. It won't run off into the forest."

"But I would, given half a chance."

"What are you waiting for? Let's go."

We set off for the distant forest. On the way we swiped salt and paper napkins from the farm's dining room. We pulled up some young potatoes and picked a few cucumbers from a field on the outskirts of the farm. I did not consider this to be theft. We never took more than what could be eaten at one sitting. In private fields we dug into the soil on one side of the potato plants and pulled off a few tubers. Then we packed the earth back, knowing that by autumn the plant would yield as many potatoes as its neighbours. Seeing the tons of fruit and vegetables that rotted away in the fields it would have been a sin not to take some.

Once we reached the forest we lit a fire in a clearing and baked our potatoes. There was no shortage of kindling in the dense and tangled undergrowth. It was good to sit by the fire. I wondered why I had hung around towns for so long. I must have forgotten that you don't need much in this life.

My companion, whose name was Yura, was not a talkative person and that suited me. I was happy just to look into the flames. The potatoes baked quickly. We pulled them out and tossed them from hand to hand until they cooled a little. They burned in the mouth but the cucumbers soothed our tongues. I decided not to return to the town.

"Yura, where are you headed?"

"Armavir. Let's go together."

"But I can't walk as fast as you."

"I'm in no hurry. Summer has only just begun. There's time enough to get there by winter."

"Let's go then."

We returned to the farm. An old Cossack woman gave us three roubles and a bottle of samogon in return for chopping wood. We asked her for an aluminium mug and an old handleless saucepan. As we left we nipped into the dining room again and pinched more salt and a glass. In the shop we bought tea, tobacco and matches. Beyond the farm we headed east, following the sun. All around us stretched plantations of apricot and cherry trees. When the day drew to a close we lay down by a stream in a grove of willows and black poplars. We fetched some hay from a field and spread it down for a bed.

Yura came from Dnepopetrovsk and had been on the road for two years. He had already been in the spets twice and wanted to avoid a prison sentence. He intended to stay in the Kuban till autumn and then head off to Central Asia. That idea appealed to me and we decided to stick together. We would stay where we were for the summer, keeping our heads down and avoiding any trouble with the law. That meant not showing our faces in towns and not stealing.

I was unable to steal in any real sense; I could never imagine breaking into someone's house or dipping into their pockets. As for other sorts of theft—well, everyone in the Soviet Union stole. Our system turned us into thieves. In other countries the most hardened thief knows in his heart of hearts that he is doing wrong. Even as he is hauled off to jail he knows that he deserves his punishment. He does not like it but he knows it is just. You have to answer for your deeds. In the USSR, however, everything was turned on its head. We thought someone a fool if he did not steal from the state. The authorities thought so too. They paid us so little that we had to steal. That way they encouraged us to get our hands as dirty as theirs. Then we were in no position to complain about them, the much greater thieves.

Everyone knew the difference between genuine theft and taking back what had been stolen from us in the first place. We were only expropriating the expropriators.

"Yura," I said aloud, "stealing might be wrong, but when the state steals freedom and takes away human dignity, then people begin to construct their own values."

Yura interrupted me: "But what if everyone invented their own values? What would we have then?"

"Chaos!"

Yura slept. I drew away from the fire so that the glow did not obscure my view of the stars. I piled up some hay and lay down. I was not drunk. There was even a drop of samogon left for the morning. Having taken care of my hair-of-the-dog no other worries occupied my mind. I began to think about how to live in a way that would have some sort of meaning. My attitude to the world around me was changing. My youthful dreams of setting the world on fire had died. I knew I would never walk to the North Pole or discover a new chemical element. On the other hand I was less disturbed by my crippled leg. I knew that strength, whether mental or physical, was a cruel and destructive force. Even if you do not intend to use your strength for evil purposes, it makes no difference in the end.

After gazing for a long time at the constellations I came to a decision: I would never again say, 'if only everyone did as I did . . . ' or 'if only everyone were like that . . . '. I had to accept that people never would be the way I wanted them to be.

I was disillusioned with humanity but I could not say I hated it. You can hate flies and cockroaches, you can love bees and cabbage pasties, but I don't see how you can love or hate people when they are all so different. The man who says 'I love people' is either a politician or a scoundrel, which are one and the same, or simply an idiot who does not know what he is talking about. In the course of my life I had come into contact with tens of thousands of human beings. Some were fine and others I would not have cared to meet in hell. Most were harmless enough. It was unlikely that I myself had caused joy to leap in many hearts.

I decided that from then on I would behave as though other people did not exist. Even when I was in a crowded bazaar I would act as though I were on a desert island. To live in and for oneself sounds very simple but in practice it is almost impossible. I was human like anyone else and affected by those around me. Added to which, as a Soviet citizen, I had drunk in the word 'we' with my mother's milk. Whether I succeeded or not, the most important thing was that I had made my decision. No one could alter it or prevent me from trying to carry it out.

Perhaps I only wanted to justify my existence, but I did not think of it like that. Let the clever chaps discover complexes according to Freud or Jung. I felt satisfied and went to sleep at last.

In the forest you can only sleep through the dawn if you are really tired. As soon as the sun starts to rise above the horizon the birds begin twittering so loudly that it is impossible to sleep. Although I had not dropped off until the early hours of the morning, I awoke feeling strangely cheerful and optimistic. I had become a slightly different person and I felt something good would happen that day.

Yura, on the other hand, was grumpy and sullen, and at first I thought that he regretted his decision to take me with him. When I got used to him I learned that he was always like that in the morning. He pulled off his socks and sniffed them, then he lay down again like a dead man until I had brewed chefir, which revived him somewhat. I asked him not to touch the samogon for a while, explaining that I feared the d.ts.

Coming out onto the main road we started hitching. We decided to go to the bathhouse in Armavir. We stank of bonfires and hay and booze. You can't get yourself clean in a river, even with soap. Besides, a steam bath was always a treat. You could say that if the medieval world rested on three whales, the tramp's rested on four: the railway station, the bazaar, the police station and the bathhouse.

A truck took us as far as the town of Kropotkin. "We'll have to make a detour here," Yura said. "The Kropotkin police chief doesn't care for tramps. Haven't you heard about him?"

I shook my head.

"He used to be a farmer. One day he insulted three tramps and in revenge they stole his geese. Then they wrote a request to Moscow radio 'on behalf of the farm labourers of Armavir' for the well-known and popular song 'Goodbye geese, goodbye!' A couple of weeks later the 500 voices of the Piatnitsky choir reminded the farmer that he had had his geese stolen. The shame might have driven a lesser man to hang himself, but this guy was made of sterner stuff. He left his farm and joined the Kropotkin police force, taking his revenge on passing tramps. Vagrants all over the country, even those in prison, still send their requests to Moscow."

Yura and I were on the road for more than a month, wandering in a circle around the Kuban. The southern earth enveloped us like a kind mother. You could not take a step without treading on a ripe apricot or a bunch of grapes. All around was a sea of corn and fields overflowing with melons that no one bothered to pick. After they had met government sowing targets farm managers relaxed and let the harvest take care of itself.

I did not listen to a radio or read a paper. I did not care whether we had cosmonauts in space or receptions for Fidel Castro. My body felt rested and my soul was at peace. No one was nagging at me to work harder or stop drinking.

Then it began to rain. For three days we hardly stuck our noses out of a haystack. The rain was chilly and incessant. Once or twice we went up to the nearest farm, where peasants gave us as much milk as we wanted. Yura drank until his stomach barrelled out so tightly you could snap fleas on it with your fingernails.

The rain got me down so I suggested we take shelter by registering ourselves on a farm. We trudged six muddy kilometres to the nearest farm administration centre and were immediately hired. Yura was to tend the cattle while I, as an invalid, and having no documents except a certificate of graduation from the Novorossisk spets, was hired as a watchman. I also had to drive the carthorses out from the stables when the farmers needed to take goods to market. My duty was to walk around at night, shooting in the air to scare off the stray dogs trying to dig up carcasses of diseased cattle from the burial pit.

The cattle lived in terrible conditions. They did not have enough to eat because feed was expensive. If they were fed at all, it was only because the farmers felt pity for the animals. It smote your heart to hear three hundred cows mooing from hunger while the cowhands lay paralytically drunk. On spring mornings farmers tipped sugar beets onto the still-frozen earth of the cattle pen. The starving cows pushed and shoved to get at the food. When the sun rose and softened the ground the animals wallowed up to their bellies in mud and excrement. Cows trampled their own calves into the filth. Still, they were not my responsibility, and my job was easy enough.

The local Cossacks treated us cautiously at first. Like all country people they did not broadcast their scandals to strangers. I soon noticed they stole everything they could carry. At five in the morning they stumbled out of their huts, stuffing empty bags into their pockets. They piled into buses which roared off down the sawdust-strewn road. In the evenings they returned with bags full of feed, corn cobs, or what ever else they had been able to lay their hands on. It was said that a wife would not serve her husband dinner unless he brought at least a couple of planks or a piece of fencing back with him from work.

Looking at me sympathetically, one of the Cossack women sighed, "Oh, you poor man!"

"And why do you say that?"

"How do you survive with a leg like that?"

"I get by; always have and always will."
"But you can't ride a bicycle."
"Why the hell would I want to do that?"
"But you can't carry much away on foot!"
"But I don't need anything."

She gaped at me as though I were a simpleton. Later I learned that the first thing any peasant did was buy himself a bicycle. Then he would go to the driver of a combine harvester, slip him three roubles and fill up a bag of cut corn cobs. One sack was hard to carry over the shoulder, but two or three could be hung from a bike. He could sell the corn in the market for 15 roubles, making the bicycle a machine for printing money. If he did well he would use his profits to buy a motorbike with a side car, and thus steal a lot more.

They say that if you stick a shaft in the Kuban soil in spring you will have a cart growing by autumn. But this fertile agricultural region was going to waste because of the collective farm system. The more intelligent peasants left the farm for the towns; the more artful joined the Party and sat at conferences where they assured each other that everything was under control. The simpler people stayed put and drank everything they could lay their hands on.

It is not true that people only work for money. If someone is paid to dig a hole every day and fill it in again, he might work for a while but in the end he will rebel; that is why seventy years of communism produced 200 million thieves and drunkards.

I slept in a five-room hut with four other single down-and-outs, plus three families who had been in the same situation themselves in the very recent past.

One of these consisted of a couple of drug addicts we nicknamed Codeine and Codeina. This pair wandered around the farm like somnambulists. They had a baby who slept all the time, perhaps addicted through its mother's milk. How he grew up God alone knows. He probably did not, unwanted as he was. The couple were supposed to work in the chicken sheds. At night when the birds were blind, Codeina would grab half a dozen, bind their beaks with thread and take them off to Slavyansk to trade for pills with pharmacists.

Codeine took alternate shifts with me as a night watchman. He often came over to play cards with us and drink chefir. He gave out pills to those he trusted. The codeine made us scratch ourselves frantically.

Amongst us was a young man who was hiding out on the farm—reasons were not asked. Born a Carpathian peasant, he understood everything that concerned agriculture; as regards anything else, he was as thick as a tree stump. Seeing us scratch ourselves, he would go into the next room and examine his clothes carefully for lice.

One day I awoke after a long card session and stumbled out of the hut. I bumped into Klava, a neighbour from another hut.

"Hey Klava, what's the time?"

"Eight," she replied.

"How come?" I asked in surprise. I could see by the sun that it was already later than that.

"With me it's always eight o'clock," Klava bellowed, turning her back to me, bending over and lifting her skirts; between her bare buttocks she presented me with two holes, one above the other like a figure eight.

Every day Klava and her husband battled each other with pitchforks and mallets. The most surprising thing is that neither managed to kill the other. When drunk Klava would burst into our rooms, throw off our blankets and try to climb onto one of us. I kept a hoe by my bed to drive her away. When the lads rejected her advances she stood outside cursing and throwing stones at our windows.

As a Heroine Mother of the USSR Klava did not have to work. Her husband turned up in the fields now and again, just to see what he might steal. The couple had countless children. The little ones crawled around the farm, putting everything from apricots to dog shit in their mouths.

Still, I was in no position to judge my neighbours. I drank every day. Samogon was as copious as the waters of the Volga. The local peasants distilled it from tobacco. In the morning it made your head ache unbearably, so you had to take a hair-of-the-dog immediately.

I felt as though I was being sucked into quicksand. A little while longer and I would never be able to tear myself away from Red Shaft Collective Farm. My pay was better than it had been in any chemical factory, and there was not much work to do. I enjoyed plentiful food, lots to drink and girls as sweet and strong as apples.

The girls came to us from the Cossack village of Petrovka, which lay twelve kilometres to the south. They had their fun with us away from the eyes of their fathers and brothers. In their community they counted for very little; since early childhood they had had to work like donkeys. The breadth and strength of their arms deceived anyone who wanted to be deceived. Sometimes in the morning I discovered that the girl I had spent the night with was not even 16 years old.

While bringing the horses in one day I got caught in a storm. In a few seconds I was soaked to the skin and I developed pneumonia. The farm's doctor wanted to take me to hospital, but I refused.

"You will be dead by tonight," she threatened.

"All to the good. Maybe spoons will be cheaper then," I replied.

"Do you know what you are saying?" she asked.

"Yes. I have to shit, and you are preventing me."

She withdrew. Somehow I made it to the bucket my friends had supplied and then I slept. In the morning I awoke feeling weak but well and flooded with happiness. I had a strong urge to visit my daughter in Estonia.

A week later I left the collective farm, taking only the watch they had awarded me for my labour. I did not even collect my wages. Money frightened me.

chapter nine

I wanted to see Daisy before she forgot who I was, so I set off for Estonia. A tractor drove me to Slavyansk, and there I walked to the station. The conductor of a westbound express was happy to give me a berth in exchange for my Red Shaft watch. I travelled as far as Rostov; after that I made my way northwards on local trains to Taganrog, and across the Ukraine through the Donbass and then back into Russia through Belgorod, Kursk, Oryol and Tula. As I travelled I kept an eye on schoolboys who always knew when the conductor was on his way. When the train halted and they jumped off I would limp along after them, climbing into carriages that had already been checked. All the same, I was caught a few times and put off the train. Then I would have to wait for hours on some draughty station for the next local train to pull in.

The whole way I kept as sober as glass and on constant lookout for the police. My jacket was only distinguishable from a convict's by its collar, my shoes were falling apart and I sprouted a beard. I had only to step into a waiting room for the attention of all uniforms to fasten upon me like a magnet. In Tula I was accosted by a guardian of law and order: "Where are you going?" he asked.

"Home."

"And where's 'home'?"

"The collective farm."

"Which collective farm would that be?"

"What do you mean 'which'?" I looked at him with the eyes of Saint Francis. "Ours!"

I told myself not to overdo it, for the policeman had probably left the collective farm himself not so long ago.

"And where is *your* farm?" he asked, spitting out the words as though they were pieces of shit in his mouth.

"It's in the Kuban," I answered, putting on a Ukrainian accent.

"Do you have your documents?"

"Well of course!" I proudly declared and brought out a package wrapped in old newspaper. The policeman looked on with distaste as I pulled off the paper. My new passport was already stained and the residence permit almost illegible.

"It's my fault," said I, "but I did not know that it was leaking."

"What was?"

"The lamp!"

"What lamp?"

"The kerosene one. The electrician was drunk and burnt the transformer."

"Get the hell out of here! If I see your stupid face again you'll go straight into the spets."

So I continued northwards, trying to ride by night when ticket controllers were sleepy. By day I wandered around towns, collecting empty bottles for a couple of roubles to buy bread. I bummed cigarettes, or picked up dog ends and rolled them in newspaper. Sometimes I would share a cigarette with another vagrant, sitting by his side smoking in silence, feeling as close as brothers.

I reached Moscow, crossed the city, and that same day I was heading northwards. As I neared my destination, however, my courage began to fail. I longed to see Daisy, but I did not know whether she would be pleased to see her father, especially in his beard and filthy clothes. At Bologoye I had to wait a whole day for an Estonia-bound train. I sat on the cold platform lost in thought. Suddenly I rose, crossed the footbridge and took the next train south. I returned to Moscow and then jumped trains to Tambov, Rostov and finally to Sochi. I was relieved that I had made my decision in time. If I had gone to see Daisy I might have done irreparable harm.

"Kind people! Answer me anyone who hears!"

"What do you want?" I called out.

A blind man tapped his way towards my voice. His face was exactly as I imagined Blind Pew's in *Treasure Island*. He did not wear dark glasses, perhaps because he wanted people to see the terrible livid scarring around his eyes.

"Brother!" he cried, "Help me get a bottle. I can hear a whole crowd of people around me. I shall be trampled."

Not waiting for my reply, he started to pour small coins from his pocket into his cap. "Don't worry," he murmured, "the shopgirl will be glad of the change. Get us a couple of bottles."

"But I haven't enough for a bottle myself."

"What are you talking about? Take as much as you need! And a bit extra for yourself. My trousers are sagging with the weight. Perhaps you need it all?"

I came out of the shop with three bottles and caught up with Blind Pew on the corner. With his cap held out to passers-by he whined, "Help me good people. I was burned in a tank at the battle of Kursk."

"I see you waste no time," I said.

"Ah, you're back. Well, what are you standing around for—slurping up the snot dripping from your nose? Where shall we drink?"

"It's all the same to me."

Pew led me off, directing me to left and right, until we reached an obscure beer stall tucked away under a railway bridge. They knew him there and immediately laid out glasses for us. Placing a finger across the rim of each glass in turn, Pew carefully poured the wine.

"I grew up in Sochi. I was blinded a few years ago when I fell into a pit of quicklime. Usually I take someone along with me to keep an eye out for the police and to buy bottles. I used to have a girlfriend but the police picked her up in Sukhumi.

"The cops can't do much except give me a kicking, but I'm scared of being sent to the invalid home—that's worse than a strict regime prison. They take your pension and feed you worse than in camp. The staff steal all the food. Anyone who still has their legs runs away.

"Of course if you live rough you're always caught between two flames. In railway stations there are plenty of folk around, but you have to look out for the police. In quiet places you get beaten up and robbed by thugs. They know we won't run screaming to the law. Anyway, where are you headed?"

"Central Asia," I said.

"Why not stick around with me? You'll see how much we can make in a day."

"Sorry, I've made my mind up. The police here are getting on my nerves.'

"Well I want to go to Sukhumi to find my lady friend. Let's go together."

I agreed out of curiosity. Sukhumi lay in the right direction.

After we had finished the wine we went to work. Blind Pew directed me to the centre of town and told me to stop outside the department store. Taking off his cap and putting a sombre expression on what was left of his face, he began to sing:

"The bright moon shone
Over the old graveyard
And the judge wept
by a grey tombstone."

A crowd gathered to hear the sad song of a boy sentenced to death by his own father. I walked from one street corner to the other keeping a lookout for the cops. From time to time Blind Pew tipped his takings into his pocket so that people did not think he was making too much. When he pointed his index finger downwards it meant it was time for a smoke break. Finally Pew said, "Greed killed the friar, let's stop now."

We fortified ourselves with wine and counted our takings. A Moscow diva would have envied us. We had made thirty roubles in two hours.

"But you only sing one song," I complained.

"It's the only one I can remember."

We bought some bottles for the night. I took Pew home to the basement where I had been dossing, but that turned out to be a mistake; his snores must have woken everyone on the floor above, for in the early hours of the morning the police arrived and hauled us off. Luckily we received nothing worse than a beating. They gave us 24 hours to leave Sochi.

Reaching the station, we walked along a platform and forced open the pneumatic doors of an local train. We lay down in an empty carriage and Pew was soon snoring again. A couple of hours later the train jerked and began to move, taking us towards Sukhumi. I checked the adjoining carriage before returning to give Pew the all clear. He stumbled down the carriage, singing a song I had taught him the night before, one I remembered from my childhood:

Allow me to introduce myself:
my name is Nikolai Bottle

*Everyone points their fingers
and calls me 'drunk' and 'wastrel.'*

*At work they all laugh:
"Look at Bottle drunk again!"
The boss picks on me
but I'll make him pay!*

*Again the d.ts torture me,
my family's gone; the street's my life.
Vodka is my only friend,
Who introduced us? My wife!*

*I do not stand with hand outstretched,
But I walk through the bazaar
Shouting: Good people—buy my soul!
but who wants the soul of a drinker?*

My song was a success; people laughed and gave Pew money and a glass of chacha[1]. I made no sign that I knew him.

By the time we reached Sukhumi Pew was rejoicing over the money he had made. He asked me to accompany him further, explaining he would have forgotten the song by tomorrow morning and would need me to teach it to him again.

I declined. I felt begging was degrading; besides, I did not want to be supported by Pew. When we alighted at Sukhumi he directed me to the bazaar. A group of alkashi were gathered by the entrance. One of

---

[1] Chacha is a Georgian spirit made with grape-skins.

them, a bloated, ragged woman, screeched when she saw Pew. Detaching herself from her comrades she ran up and flung her arms around him. Together they staggered off to the station to work the train again.

I wandered off to try my luck in town. It was my first time in Georgia and I felt out of place. People were dressed better than in Russia, and I felt they were looking down their noses at me. I spent the day wandering through the town drinking nothing but Turkish coffee. The streets were full of men kissing each other and talking across every doorway[2]. Many people wore photos of their dead on their lapels and most women wore mourning. When two men began talking behind me I stepped to one side thinking a fight was about to break out. Cars careered about like rabid dogs, paying little attention to lights. Drivers stopped to talk to their friends, ignoring the angry queue behind them

When I had spent the money Blind Pew left me I wandered back to the bazaar. Thinking to make a bit of cash I picked up a woman's basket of peppers.

"If we see you again you'll spend the rest of your life working to buy medicine," a fierce voice suddenly growled in my ear.

Behind him, a group of Kurds were glowering at me. There was nothing left to do but get the hell out of there.

I had not gone far before a pot-bellied policemen hissed at me through his gold teeth: "You, Vassya! Come here!"

'That's the end of my wandering,' I thought.

[2] Talking across a threshold is considered bad luck in Russia.

The police station was piled to the ceiling with confiscated mandarins. Three other vagrants were loading them into cars. I was told to help them. When we were done the cops gave us each five roubles and a bottle of chacha. I walked out of the station shaking my head in bewilderment. "I won't be able to tell anyone about this," I said to one of the other tramps. "They'll take me for a compulsive liar. Russian police would sooner hang themselves with their own belts than behave like that."

It was not long before a dark man approached me and asked, "Want a job Vassya?"

"What sort of job?"

"Building a fence—three or four days."

"How much?"

"Ten roubles a day and drink."

"Where do you want me to go?"

"To the village. I'll take you there and back," the man replied, pointing to a car.

I hadn't much choice. It was dark when we arrived in the man's village. He took me to his farm and directed me to a large shed where bunches of bay leaves and eucalyptus were drying. I lay down and slept in the sweet-scented air. I was warned not to smoke for a spark could send the whole place up in flames.

For three days I dug holes, set posts into them and strung up barbed wire. The wire scratched and tore my hands, even through gloves. An old man lived in the house with three huge dogs. In the evening he put out flagons of wine and chacha for me. I did not touch the chacha for I knew that once I started I would never finish the work.

While I was stretching out the wire I saw a Russian working in a neighbouring field. He came over.

"I've been here two months," he said. "They give me all the chacha I want but they never seem to have any money to pay me. Each morning I have to work for my hair-of-the-dog. I finish the bottle in the evening. I can't seem to find a way out."

The old man saw us talking and suddenly called me over: "Police coming," he said, making signs that I would be arrested.

"Okay," I replied, "give me my money and I'll leave."

"No monny, my son bring monny tomorrow."

I almost cried with rage. I had ripped up my hands for nothing. I knew that if I left without my pay I would resent it for the rest of my life. The old man stood watching me, surrounded by his dogs and I saw in his eyes that he was laughing at me. There was nothing I could say to him. Unexpectedly even to myself I went into the barn, grabbed my things and cried out, "If I don't see my money in five minutes I'll burn the place down!"

I showed him the box of matches in my fist.

The old man immediately found the money. Fearing his dogs, I grabbed a pitchfork, throwing it away only after I had left the farm and was boarding a local bus.

At Sukhumi station I joined up with another 'Vassya', a tubercular lad named Artur. We discussed the difficulties of working in the Caucasus.

"Never work for an Azerbaijani," said Artur. "When it comes to settling up, blood drips from their teeth. I spent three months working for one of them last autumn. He was supposed to pay me five roubles a day.

I finished my work as agreed, but he drove me away, waving a knife and threatening me with the police. I crept back at night. The dogs knew me so they did not make a noise. I cut down all their fruit trees and ran off. Greed played a sour joke on those people.

"It's worse in the mountain villages where the Svan people live. They lock you up at night. If you try to escape they'll cut one of your fingers off. Even if you make them pay up the villagers take the money back as you leave. What can you do when you are alone? They all know each other and the police are their cousins. Yes brother, it's real slavery up there.

"It's true no one forces us to work in the mountains, but we can't earn anything in town. When someone wants to hire me I say to them, 'I'll work for you, only no skullduggery! I have no house or car to lose; you won't have either if I don't get my pay!

"But I must say there are some really stupid tramps. Some of them only take jobs so they can nose around looking for something to steal. They grab whatever they can find, run off, sell it, and get picked up right away at the nearest beer stall."

I did not stay long in Sukhumi as I feared the old man's son might find me. I went back to Sochi and my old haunts.

My legs felt tired after drinking for the whole morning. The pie woman had gone off to lunch so I went over to sit down on her stool by her stall. Holiday-makers strolled past on their way to the beach. Suddenly a lad detached himself from his group: "What are you selling here, uncle?"

"Jokes!" I replied.

"How much are they?" he asked in an exaggerated peasant accent.

"Roub' each," I answered in the same tone.

"So much!"

"Why, I'm almost giving them away. Roub' if you don't know the joke and I'll give you a roub' if it's already grown a beard."

"Go on then!" cried the lad, and his group gathered around my stall. I was heavily under the influence of Bacchus and quickly earned 15 roubles, not because my jokes were so good but because the youths were in high spirits and pleased to be entertained.

The next day, after drinking my hair-of-the-dog, I went to collect the baggage I had left behind in spring. Much to my surprise, the man who was looking after it had not sold all my things, although there was not much left. He gave me a small rucksack in exchange for my suitcase. Into this I put underwear, photographs, two novels and a cloth-bound exercise book in which I wrote the crosswords that I liked to devise during my sober periods.

I set off for Central Asia, where work was easier to find. Luckily most of the trains ran at night so I was able to sleep on them and spend the days wandering around Sukhumi, Samtredia, Tblisi and Kirovbad. I travelled without tickets. Although I had money I thought it as absurd to pay for a ticket as it would have been to drive my own Mercedes.

Baku reminded me of Central Asian cities, with its cafes serving black tea in tiny narrow-waisted glasses. But I was not interested in tea. From first thing in the morning I was drinking beer and the local Agdam fortified wine.

After quenching my thirst I leaned against a wall to watch the local people. A passer-by stopped to pick up a crumb of bread which someone had dropped onto the ground. The man pressed the crumb to his lips and placed it on top of the wall. "So the birds can reach it more easily," he said, seeing my astonished stare. "In Azerbaijan we respect bread, my friend."

In the bazaar I made the acquaintance of some local tramps and together we earned 15 roubles loading a trailer with oranges. Learning that I had nowhere to spend the night they invited me to come with them. "We have a splendid place. Safe as a tank and warm as a bathhouse. The police don't check it as it is in the basement of officers' flats."

Having bought several bottles we took the tram across town to our lodging place. We descended to the basement of the flats. Opening a thick steel door, we clambered quickly over some central heating pipes, so hot they turned spit into steam. The shelter was as dark as the Pharaoh's tomb. My new friends lit candles and drank themselves to sleep.

I spent the whole night awake, sitting in total darkness after the candles guttered out. I had not had enough to drink; it took a lot to give me a couple of hours' oblivion. In this state I dared not even close my eyes or the nightmares would begin. The air around me was heavy with foreboding. 'This is how animals must feel before an earthquake,' I thought. My new acquaintances snored happily while I sat goggling into the darkness. I could hear rats running about. They were not part of my nightmare, for I heard one of my sleeping friends wake with a shout of pain: "Swine! They don't let me sleep. We'll have to bring some sausage tomorrow or they will grow too bold altogether!" He dropped off again.

I thought the night would never end. When a radio in the flat above us began to broadcast morning exercises I felt as joyful as if I had seen the second coming of Christ. We crawled out of the basement and I parted from my acquaintances forever. "Lads, if that basement were stacked with vodka and it was thirty degrees below outside you'd only get me back in there under armed escort."

"And what did you expect—the Astoria?"

"But it's full of rats!"

"So what? Did they eat you alive?"

"Who knows what was on their fucking minds—I'm not hanging around to find out."

I wandered off to the port. Sailors stood by the gangplanks of Caspian ferries attentively checking tickets. I was turned back a couple of times as I tried to sneak aboard. An Azerbaijani noticed my unsuccessful efforts and approached me: "Do you want to earn the price of a bottle?"

"What must I do for it?"

"Carry these two suitcases on board this ferry. Your hands will be full so you can tell the controller that someone behind you has your ticket."

I looked at the two suitcases doubtfully. They seemed too large for me to carry.

"Pick them up, give them a try," urged the Azerbaijani, seeing my doubt.

They were extraordinarily light. "What's in them, cotton wool?"

"Walnuts."

The Azerbaijani had been kicked out of Baku by the local police after being stung for 50 roubles for illegal trading. I picked up the cases and boarded the ship without any trouble.

When we docked at Krasnovodsk in Turkmenistan I helped the man unload his cases. As we stepped ashore cops surrounded us. The Baku police must have radioed ahead to their Turkmeni colleagues who had now come to collect their bribe. Ignoring me, they took the Azerbaijani to the station, leaving me with a large bag of nuts. After waiting several hours for him I went to the market and sold my booty for 80 roubles. That was a great piece of good fortune.

In the evening I went to the station and caught a train to Tashkent, slipping the carriage conductor some money. Like all conductors in Asia he regarded the railway as his personal fiefdom, except when it came to cleaning, for then it belonged to the state.

Beyond the windows I saw nothing but desolation. The desert may be lovely in spring, but this was winter and there was nothing but an expanse of grey dunes stretching between horizons, unrelieved by grass or bushes. Occasionally the train halted by a few wretched clay hovels with mangy camels tethered behind them.

Although Ashkhabad means beloved city it does not deserve the name. In the autumn of 1948 it was destroyed by an earthquake so severe that only one building remained undamaged. The town was built afresh, with buildings no higher than three stories.

They looked as though they had been hatched from the same incubator. The streets were only slightly less depressing than in Krasnovodsk for some were lined with trees; however this was December, so it made no difference.

At the station buffet I fell in with a local alkie called Kerya. Together we banished our hangovers with a bottle of wine and then went down to the Tekinskii bazaar. The stock exchange, as the bazaar was called, was a lively place where local alkies congregated. It was easy enough to earn a couple of roubles hauling baskets of apples. As soon as we had a few coins in our hands we took care of our drinking requirements. Only after that did we think of food. We helped ourselves to apples, capsicums, Chardzhou melons, and dipped our dirty paws into great barrels of marinated garlic.

Kerya showed me a bunch of keys in his possession. "These will open all 64 flats in a new apartment block," he proudly said. "It was built by Bulgarians in an international friendship project. I stole the keys from a drunken builder. It's still empty. I've already slept a few nights there. Come home with me. You'll sleep like a lord."

The 'Bulgarian' building protected us from the 20 degree frost outside, but I grew sick of Kerya's company. Drink was his only topic of conversation.

"Where do the other tramps sleep?" I asked. "Do the cops make up feather beds for them in the railway station?"

"Not likely. If they catch you sleeping there they give you a good going over, and if the same cop catches you twice you get a month for sure."

Kerya screwed up his eyes like a contented cat and added, "I had to sleep in a basement for nearly three months before I got hold of these keys!"

He reminded me of the legendary Volga tramp who found himself a place under an upturned boat on the beach. Graciously inviting another tramp to come in and doss down beside him, he placed a pile of dog ends before the man: 'Have a smoke, brother, don't be shy. I was in your position myself not so long ago.'

"Where did you sleep before you got the keys?" I asked, wanting to prolong this rare conversation.

"Want me to show you?"

"Why not? There's nothing else to do."

Off we went, picking up a few bottles on the way with the remains of my walnut money. Kerya took me to a block of flats and led me down to the basement. Although it was night the scene below was as bright as day, lit by a bonfire of burning tyres. A group of people were sitting around the bonfire, women as well as men. Their faces were covered in hideous weeping sores produced by a tropical disease rife in Turkmenia. The filth in which the tramps lived spread the infection. When the sores healed they left a deep scar. It was hard enough to behold children suffering from the disease, but the tramps looked repulsive.

Nevertheless I was pleased at the thought of company so I sat down and produced my bottles. The basement dwellers welcomed me as though I were Santa Claus. I was already three sheets to the wind when we arrived, and after a top-up I felt such a sense of brotherhood with the tramps that I invited them all to our Bulgarian house. Kerya dropped into a few more basements on the way back. Soon we were about fifty people. We stocked up as we went; every bottle-peddling pensioner on every street corner must have made a profit that night.

Our Bulgarian house was soon blazing with light and rocking with noise as though it were a Caribbean cruiser gone off course in the night. Some of our guests sang; others remembered old offences. Glass windows shattered and curses echoed through the rooms. The police arrived before anyone could be killed and drove us out of the building. They enthusiastically hit us with their truncheons but seemed reluctant to arrest us. They probably feared contagion. In the confusion I managed to slip away, making my way back to the station. I had had enough of Ashkhabad.

As the train slowed to a halt between Artik and Dushak I asked a soldier on the platform, "Can I get off for a smoke?"

With a bored gesture, he indicated the exit with the barrel of his Kalashnikov. However, as soon as my feet touched the ground, he shouted, "Stop! I am arresting you for breaking frontier regulations." He pointed a revolver at my head.

A sergeant came running up and helped escort me to a separate carriage. There was another man already in the carriage. The soldiers locked us in and left. I pulled two bottles of wine from my rucksack and gave one to my companion. We drank quickly before the soldiers returned.

Border guards were recruited from the keenest Komsomol activists, the type of person who will happily inform on his colleagues. Someone must have told an officer that we had got drunk after our arrest. At Dushak the interrogating officer asked me about this very persistently. The soldier who had arrested me stood by his side looking so miserable that I took pity on him and said that I had already been drunk when I stepped off the train.

Then the officer pointed to my notebook of crosswords. "What are these?"

"Crosswords; I make them up."

"Why?"

"It passes the time. I sent one to Smena once," I babbled, "but they rejected it with apologies. They said one of my words was derived from Church Slavonic."

"Hmm . . . Why were you trying to cross the Soviet border?"

"Who me? Do I look like a madman? I don't know a word of Farsi and I can't run."

The officer glanced at my leg. I sensed that he did not believe I was guilty. However, once the wheels of justice were in motion, there was no going back.

'Let's hope no one trod on the judge's foot in the bus,' I thought to myself on the morning of my trial. The length of my sentence would depend on the judge's mood. It was clear I was not an Iranian spy, but I was a vagrant and idleness was a crime against the very foundation of the Soviet state.

My trial lasted a few minutes. I refused my right to a final word and this probably pleased the judge, allowing him to get away to his lunch. He gave me a year of strict regime prison with compulsory treatment for alcoholism. There was no hope of remission. I was not overjoyed with this sentence, but neither was I tearing my hair out. By this time I knew I could survive camp; I only had to remember not to think myself smarter than the others or get mixed up in other people's business. If I shared my tobacco down to the last roll-up and refused to give way to self pity, then prison life would be tolerable. Still, I felt apprehensive as I awaited my transfer, wondering what my fellow inmates would be like.

chapter ten

"I used to have a friend called Kuzya who rode a bicycle better than anyone else, although he had not a single tooth in his head. Kuzya's father, Uncle Kostya, was an electrician, and an excellent one too. When he took two leads in his hands and screwed a lightbulb in his arse it shone twice as bright as usual. Strangely enough, Uncle Kostya was electrocuted by a car accumulator which fell on his head as he was walking down the street one day. The accumulator came from a Moskvich 412.

"I have to say that misfortune dogged that family. Their cow Milka once farted so violently that her horns straightened out. It could have had something to do with the fact that Kuzya's brother Prokhor was molesting her at the time. He was a real hooligan.

"When Uncle Kostya was killed they decided to make a wake such as Russian folk held in the old days. They slaughtered Milka to make dumplings from her, but again a misfortune occured. Auntie Frosya, who was Kuzya's mother, was senile, poor woman. As she put the meat through the mincer one of her breasts got caught and was pulled off from the shoulder. Afterwards the guests to a man praised the dumplings and said they had never tasted anything like them, but they could not quite identify the meat.

"The only upstanding member of that family was Nastya, Kuzya's elder sister. She was remarkable for her extraordinary cleanliness. Every day she went down to the bathhouse, although not to the communal chamber like everyone else, but to a private room. It is true that each time she went in with a different man, but I don't think that makes any difference. In the evening she used to sit quietly and count her money. I cannot say exactly but it seems to me that she worked as a cashier."

The prisoner we called Death Number Two paused in full flow and glared at me: "Hey, slurper! Are you from Kolyma or what?"

I shook my head. The way you drank your chefir revealed your camp history. 'Kolyma' drinkers swallowed their chefir in three gulps; 'Norilsk' drinkers in two.

"Never mind, let's have another brew," and Death Number Two picked up his teapot and ran over to the Titan boiler in the corner of our workshop. He rinsed the pot, poured in some hot water, sprinkled in a large heap of green tea and ran back to his bench to put the lid on before the tea had cooled. We huddled together in a circle, smoking rough tobacco rolled in newspaper while we waited for the chefir to brew. The anticipation was even better than the chefir itself. When it was ready Death carefully filled a bowl and poured it back into the teapot, so that the leaves settled and did not get into our mouths.

"Have a punch in the liver, Vanya," Death said as he handed me a cup.

I had to dope myself with chefir or I would not have been able to do a day's work. I felt like death myself when I awoke in the morning. My head and muscles ached, my guts churned and my skin crawled. After a few mouthfuls of chefir I returned to life. I teamed up with a group of fellow chefirists, for only the very strong or the completely despised could survive on their own.

The huge workshop buzzed like a million beehives. Dust and tobacco smoke hung so thick in the air you could see no further than ten metres. The midday heat rose to 45 degrees so everyone stripped to the waist. Bodies gleamed with sweat as they bent over their sewing machines.

I worked on my own machine, making gloves. This was almost freedom as it saved me from the production line. I could work at my own pace and it was not hard to meet the quota of 72 pairs a day. My pay went straight to the camp for my keep. The few roubles I earned for exceeding the quota paid for tobacco and tea. Prisoners with wealth and influence bought their quota from other zeks. Freed from the obligation to work, they lounged about smoking opium and hashish.

Most of Ashkhabad's 1,500 inmates took opium. It was brought in by visitors, delivery men, or sometimes thrown over the fence at a pre-arranged spot. Even the guards would bring in drugs for a large enough bribe. Indian hemp grew in the camp yard. As soon as the buds appeared they were picked, dried and smoked in joints.

You could buy drugs in the camp bazaar along with anything else you needed. Zek traders set up stalls outside the barracks and sold envelopes, stamps, tobacco, tea, socks and even tomatoes, potatoes and rice. Some of the Turkmen zeks never used the canteen, prefering to cook their own pilaus on bonfires outside the barracks. You could always supplement your diet with cans of condensed milk, traded for opium by tubercular addicts who had climbed over the fence from the hospital zone.

The Turkmen and Uzbeks swallowed their opium with green tea. Sometimes they speared a ball of it on some wire and heated it over a flame. Then they inhaled the smoke with their heads under a newspaper funnel. When a powerful Turkmen was due to be released he would cook up a big pilau and stir in opium and hashish. Friends took their turns with the spoon in a strict pecking order.

One day an old Turkmen was brought into our cell. As soon as the guards had left he shuffled into a corner, squatted down and began to sing endless plaintive Turkmen dirges. As he sang he swayed back and forth on his heels, sometimes so violently that he keeled over onto the floor. He seemed to be a lunatic, but we began to suspect that the old Turkmen *babai* was in fact as high as a kite. Everyone racked their brains trying to work out how he got hold of his drugs. He would have been carefully searched so he could not have brought them in from the outside. We kept a close watch on the old man and noticed that every so often he would break off his lament, chew on the sleeves of his caftan, then roll his eyes heavenwards and resume his keening. After hours of questioning he confided in another Turkmen zek that he had been forewarned of his arrest, so he had prepared himself by boiling up opium and soaking his clothes in the solution.

When the rest of the cell discovered the secret of the babai they tore his caftan off, ripped it into pieces and ate them. For two days everyone was off their heads. I also tried a bit but it had little effect on me; I had not cultivated a taste for opium.

"Death," I said to my friend the next day, "it seems the Turkmen can sing for 24 hours a day and about anything at all. If one sees a camel train passing, he will sing,

'The first camel goes by,
The second goes by,
The third goes by . . . '

When the whole train has passed he sings,

'And at the back a little camel goes by,
And blood drips from his hooves.
Oh! If only someone could see him!
They would weep tears of pity!'

"I have never heard one cheerful song. They are all mournful."

"Ah," replied Death, "people say the Italians are the songbirds of the world, but they are nothing compared to the Turkmen. They don't speak much; their philosophy is all in their songs."

Most of Ashkhabad's inmates had been sentenced for drug-related crimes. Almost every Central Asian adult smoked hashish but there were far fewer addicts among them than amongst the Russians and other

Europeans. For centuries the locals used hashish and raw opium, but widespread addiction only appeared with the Russians.

As most of Turkmenistan is desert, drugs were brought in from Kyrgyzia, which has a more favourable climate for hemp and poppies. Whole villages were devoted to their cultivation. Smugglers also brought in drugs from Iran and Afghanistan. The mafia never carried stuff themselves and did not usually take drugs. Although the police were astonishingly inefficient, they had to catch a few smugglers, which made it a dangerous business. You got five years for a small quantity and 15 for larger amounts. You might even be shot. Because of the risk the mafia often used outsiders as couriers.

A man called Lazarev worked on a machine near me. Although he came from a family of Old Believers[1] he had been a tramp and an alcoholic for much of his life. Lazarev told me how he had ended up in camp.

"One day a man came up to me at a beer stall and bought me some drinks. We got talking and he asked if I wanted to make some money. 'Sure,' I said, 'how?' 'Take a suitcase to Frunze. We'll give you your ticket and the key to a locker in the station. There'll be 1,000 roubles inside.'

"Of course I had a pretty good idea what was in the case, but I asked no questions. I hoped that the money might enable me to clean up and go back home to my wife. The unknown man bought me a new suit of

---

[1] The Old Believers were a sect that broke away from the Russian Orthodox Church in the seventeenth century. Members were supposed to renounce alcohol and tobacco.

clothes and took me to the barbers. I reached Frunze without being stopped by the police. When I opened the locker I found only 200 roubles and a kilo of opium. I thought I could at least try to sell the opium, so I left the suitcase in the locker and walked out of the station. The police were waiting for me around the corner and I got eight years. The mafia have to give them occasional results.

"It would have been worse for me if I had held on to the suitcase. I did not realise then that the courier is always tailed, like in a spy story. There is a lot of money at stake. Runaway couriers are followed onto trains and when they go out to the open platform for a smoke they are pushed off. The blind Chechen in hut number four had his eyes gouged out when he tried to double-cross the mafia. After they had finished with him they handed him over to the police."

Listening to Lazarev I realised I could quite easily have been tricked in the same way. In Baku I had agreed to carry walnuts onto the ship without looking inside the cases. I had taken tomatoes from Margilan to Tashkent for the price of a ticket. I would be less naive in future.

Inside the camp the unfortunate Lazarev had become addicted to opium. He needed two balls each day, but he could never earn enough on the sewing machines to buy these. In his spare time he made syringes from small glass tubes taken from light-bulbs. The plunger was a wooden stick and the stopper was made of rubber cut from the soles of his boots. He bought needles from craftsmen who made them from tin cans in the metal workshop. Such syringes were scarce in the camp and

Lazarev was in demand. Several times a day an addict would come up to him to prepare a fix. First they put a ball of opium in an empty penicillin container, filled it with water and boiled the mixture over a burning wick. When the opium dissolved the needle was quickly inserted and the solution sucked up into the syringe. As the drug was mixed with coffee, clay and all sorts of impurities, it was filtered through a piece of cotton wool. Lazarev used to collect the cotton wool filters, boil them up and inject himself, weeping in frustration as he stabbed the needle into his ruined veins.

Conditions in the camp were filthy, so drug users dropped like flies. Addicts shared needles with syphilitics and TB sufferers. A night never passed without some deaths. In one night eighteen prisoners died from injecting adulterated drugs. The supplier was never discovered, but we all knew that the tragedy occured because the dealer had been in debt. The addicts knew the risks they were taking, but all the same almost no one came off the needle.

The most powerful zeks always knew in advance when the son of a Party family was coming in. They waited eagerly for the young innocent, ready to envelop him with care and attention. When he arrived they plied him with tobacco and tea and allowed him to win at cards. They staged situations where he was threatened by thugs so they could step in and save him. They filled him with drugs until he was convinced of his invulnerablity. Then everything came crashing down around his ears. He lost heavily at cards and his comrades insisted he pay up. He wrote home pleading for money to be sent in. As long as he could pay he survived. When they had wrung all they could from their victim the criminals left him without drugs or protection, and he would be lucky if they did not rape him as well.

The Ashkhabad Godfather needed neither the SVP nor stool pigeons. When he wanted information he put two or three of the more powerful addicts in the isolator and kept strict watch to make sure no drugs got in. In two days he would know everything. As long as the Godfather knew who was dealing drugs no one was touched. The authorities got their bribes and everything was under control. As soon as anyone stepped out of line they were punished. For example, this happened when someone tried to do a bit of dealing on the quiet and did not give a percentage to the guards.

"I want nothing more to do with drug addicts," I told Death Number Two. "I have seen enough of them in here. They act as though they have discovered some divine secret beyond the reach of ordinary mortals, as though drugs have opened their eyes and shown everything in its true light. Yet they are even more degraded than alcoholics. They are capable of any treachery just to get hold of their ball of opium.

"I am not trying to justify alcoholism. I know men who have drunk away their families, their homes and their jobs. I see one of them in the mirror every time I shave. I have heard of alkies who put their wives on the game; I have probably drunk with them."

"Their daughters too," Death Number Two casually remarked, "many female alcoholics begin their careers that way."

"But," I continued, "a drug addict would sell his mother and introduce his sister to the needle, so that she has to prostitute herself to buy drugs. The difference between us is an alkie who sells his last shirt for a bottle would not hesitate to give a glass to a friend; a drug addict would never do the same. Alkies can leave a bottle in someone's care for a while, knowing it won't be touched; no addict would let even his best friend look after his drugs—they hide their stuff away and begrudge their friends even a tiny piece. Haven't you noticed how they grow their nails long? They hope to get an extra scraping themselves, all the while eyeing their friends' nails with suspicion. No, There can be no comradeship among addicts, whereas an alcoholic will always find someone at the beer-stall to tie his belt to his glass for him, to steady his hand, or tip the glass to his trembling lips."

If I am honest I have to admit my first prison sentence was due to my pill habit, but I did not consider myself a drug addict. My passion for alcohol was enough. I would have had to take up crime to have been able to afford drugs, and I was not capable of that. Vodka, on the other hand, was always around, it was cheap and if worst came to worst, I could go without it.

Many alcoholic zeks drank 'chimirgess', which was made in the joinery shop from enamel paint. They mixed it with water and then strained it to obtain a clear liquid. Anyone who drank it went completely off his head, but if he was taken to hospital and breathalysed there would be no result. In fact there was not a drop of alcohol in chimirgess, and so I was not attracted to it.

There was a Gypsy in our work brigade called

Pashka Ogli. He was so skinny we called him 'Death Number One'. Pashka was not like the other Gypsies who were proud and kept to themselves. Everyone laughed at Pashka for his strange ways. Hearing that once upon a time aristocrats used to drink champagne from ladies' slippers he filled one of his stinking boots with chimirgess and drank it down. "As pure as tears," he sighed and collapsed in a corner.

Pashka used to stand by my machine turning gloves inside out so I could sew them more quickly. He never met his own quota but I paid him for helping me.

"Vanya," he remarked one day. "You know they watch us all the time in here. They even check the books we borrow from the library."

"Of course they don't. Maybe in some Mordvin political prisons but not in ours. They're not interested."

"You don't know what you're talking about."

He showed me volume 18 of Lenin's *Collected Works* which he had tucked into his waistband. Whenever an officer came into view, Pashka would open his Lenin, take a pencil from behind his ear and begin underlining and making exclamation marks in the margins. He would buttonhole the camp political instructor and other officers and ply them with idiotic questions about Marxist-Leninism. Soon the officers were giving Death Number One a wide berth. Everyone thought Pashka an idiot, but I was not so sure.

"See him over there?" Death Number One pointed to a strong-looking man working on a machine in the next row from ours. "He's known as 'Cannibal'. He escaped from a Kolyma camp in the 1950s. He and his mate took a fatted calf with them and killed him when their supplies ran out. They fed the young lad up before the escape. Can you imagine them, encouragingly patting him on the shoulder in order to feel the extra flesh on him. How can a man be so cynical?"

"That's not cynicism, Pashka," I replied; "someone who criticises a cannibal for not washing his hands before eating would be a cynic. There are simply no words to describe what that man did."

There is nothing special about cannibalism. People have been driven to it often enough, even in our century, during famines and the siege of Leningrad. But those were extreme situations. I was curious to know how one human being could deliberately prepare another for the slaughter. I began to chat to Cannibal after work, gradually broaching the subject that interested me.

Cannibal had spent most of his life in prison and was already in his sixth year at Ashkhabad. He did not look like a typical zek. He still had the physique of a sturdy peasant—which is what he had been before he received his first sentence for stealing wheat. Physical strength had enabled him to survive the camp mincing machine, but the experience had taught him to believe in nothing but the principle: 'You die today and I tomorrow'.

A morose man, Cannibal went about his business quietly and never initiated a conversation. He subscribed to many papers and journals, but it was useless to ask him to lend you something to read after work. In the morning yes, but come evening everything had to be in its proper place. I was never able to discover what I wanted to know. He told me his only regret was ending up in jail; everything else he had done had been justified. To all my sly questioning he simply replied, "You would have done the same in my place."

Cannibal had been behind barbed wire for so long that he had forgotten what the outside world looked like. When a modern streamlined bus drove into the zone one day he broke his usual silence by crying, "Fuck me! Would you look at that—a train without rails!"

Like Cannibal, there were many zeks who had been in camps for so long they had grown used to their loss of freedom. They felt at home behind barbed wire. Several times I saw a prisoner who had reached the end of his sentence be driven through the gates by force. One epileptic Kalmyk had no one waiting for him on the outside. He had a choice between an asylum or life on a minuscule pension. After his release he went into town and threw stones at shop windows until he was rearrested and sent back to the camp.

The Uzbeks say that beautiful dreams are half our wealth. Poor is the man who has lost his dreams or has never had any in the first place; the camps were full of such people. Many Soviet citizens, especially peasants, lived in such poor conditions that they could have swapped places with a zek without noticing any difference in their standard of living. Both prisoners and free people ate the same disgusting food; the miserable rags they wore were identical.

When I lived on the other side of the fence I had often watched people engage in petty theft while shrugging off the consequences. 'They can't send me anywhere worse than prison; they can't give me less than a pound of bread,' went the eternal refrain. When a person reaches that stage he is past caring what stupid crime he commits. Judges label as 'malicious' crimes that were commited out of simple despair by people without beautiful dreams.

Every camp inmate developed a shell around himself but few were as hardened as Cannibal. At the other end of the scale were those who could have discarded their shells quite easily if only they had been given the chance to live as a human being. One such zek was my friend Igor Alexandrovich. With his long thin head covered in prickly stubble, Igor looked like some kind of exotic cactus. There was usually a large globule of snot hanging from one of his nostrils waiting to drop off at the most inconvenient moment. Flapping his hands distractedly, Igor Alexandrovich would then fish an ancient crusted handkerchief from his pocket and dab at his nose.

We called Igor Alexandrovich by his full name and patronymic instead of by the customary nickname. He earned this exaggerated respect by his singular behaviour. Years in prison had hardly affected his speech. He rarely swore, and usually blushed when he did. He called everyone by the formal 'you', and used the old fashioned language of the pre-revolutionary intelligentsia. Igor Alexandrovich claimed his father had been an admiral who had gone over to the Bolsheviks after the revolution. Like all camp stories this was probably an exaggeration, but without a doubt Igor Alexandrovich came from a refined background. He knew quite a lot about literature, music and theatre, and you don't pick up that sort of knowledge in camp libraries. He had studied medicine in Leningrad but on graduating had been arrested and sentenced to be shot. The sentence was later transmuted to ten years.

Igor Alexandrovich was ashamed of his record and would only say that he had been imprisoned for practising illegal abortions. He had been in Kolyma and Norilsk. Because of his medical training he was put to work in camp hospitals. Thanks to that he survived.

Igor Alexandrovich was released after the 20th Party Congress, but as a former zek his diploma was no use. He went down to Central Asia where he found work in a Tashkent morgue. After he lost his job through drinking he became a tramp and beggar.

Everyone liked to listen to Igor Alexandrovich's stories and it seemed that he had come to believe his own inventions. He told us how he had always carried at least two guns of a foreign make and had lost horses, women and dachas at cards. Famous actresses had been in love with him and he had hired whole restaurants for his week-long parties.

Igor Alexandrovich found sewing difficult because of his short sight, so he never met his work quota. This meant he could not buy tobacco in the camp shop, leaving him squirming with his constant craving for a cigarette. Yet if I held out my pack to him he would refuse with elaborate excuses. So I resorted to a more devious method. I left a packet of Prima on the bench and then went to the other end of the workshop. In my absence Igor Alexandrovich tiptoed over, helped himself from my packet and slunk back to his bench. I returned to find several crushed and broken cigarettes in my pack, where they had been too hastily replaced.

From then on I resorted to this method of giving Igor Alexandrovich a smoke. Sometimes he was so overcome by shame that he dropped his precious cigarette and had to scrabble around for it amid the grease and slime of the floor.

Igor Alexandrovich enjoyed dispensing medical advice. When I cut my thumb he delivered a lengthy discourse on haemophilia: "On your release," he told me, "you should go to take the waters at a spa. Preferably Karlsbad."

"I shall certainly follow your advice," I replied.

A radio loudspeaker hung over our heads in the workshop but it was hard to hear, and anyway we were not interested in the nonsense spewed out by Moscow. One day, however, I caught the strains of an old romance: *Grief is my star*.

I switched off my machine to listen. The noise of the workshop bothered me and I glanced around in annoyance. No one else had stopped except Igor Alexandrovich, who was standing with his head stretched up towards the loudspeaker. Large tears like a child's rolled down his stubbly cheeks. I don't know where he was at that moment but he sure as hell was not in prison. I turned away so that he would not notice me looking at him.

Later Igor Alexandrovich came up to me: "Do you remember the song: *Grief is my star?*" he asked.

"Of course, but I forgot the words."

"You don't need to remember them. Words only give a song it's shape. When you love something very much its form has no significance. All lovers know this."

Igor Alexandrovich was released several months before me and the camp was a sadder place without him.

On my release I intended to wait in the town until the following day when Death Number Two would come out. We planned to head for the Kuban where Death had some relations who might give us work. However, the camp authorities had other ideas, and they put me straight onto a train to Krasnovodsk, that most desolate of cities.

I had not been out of Ashkhabad for 24 hours before I was robbed of my documents. While waiting in Krasnovodsk for Death I met an alkash with a cruel hangover. I invited him for a drink. While we were seeing off our third half-litre he suddenly crowned me with a bottle and went through my pockets as I lay out cold. At least I had had the foresight to hide my money in a pouch under my collar. I was not badly hurt but a few splinters of glass embedded themselves in my scalp. 'Well, old son,' I thought to myself, 'they say you are never too old to learn, but it seems you'll remain a fool till you die. Choose your drinking partners more carefully in future.'

I thought it better not to wait for Death any longer. Without my release papers any cop could stop me and send me back to camp. Besides, I wanted to get out of Krasnovodsk. It was winter and the town was scoured by a cruel, sand-laden wind. I took a ferry to Baku and then a train to Tblisi.

According to legend, Bogdan Khmelnitski of the Ukraine once summoned all the vagabonds in his kingdom to Kiev. He ordered straw of the best quality to be spread for them on the city's main square. When the tramps arrived they laid themselves gratefully down and went to sleep. Then Khmelnitski ordered the straw to be lit around the edges. As their bed blazed the tramps called out, "We are burning! Save us!" but none lifted a finger to help themselves. When the flames began to lick his feet their chief shouted, "How lazy you are, brothers! Why don't you cry out that I too am on fire?"

Soviet railway stations were like that square in Kiev. Their warmth and 24 hour beer stands lured us tramps like wasps to a jamjar, making it easy for the police to pick us up. We were aware of the danger but it made no difference. In Tblisi I spent a few days hanging around the staton, drinking in the buffet and trying to snatch a few hours sleep in dark corners. Eventually my luck ran out. I was arrested and taken to the spets.

My cell was crammed with bare bunks. Its lightbulb burned around the clock as the small barred window let in no sun. I had been drinking heavily for the past few days and feared the horrors would come while I was alone in the cell with no mental distractions.

"Hey, boss, give us a paper to read," I asked the sergeant when he brought my dinner. As I was being led to my cell I had noticed a pile of newspapers on a shelf in the corridor.

"They're old papers," said the sergeant.

"So what if they are; I am bored to death," I insisted.

"Do you really want something to read?"

"Well I'm not going anywhere in a hurry."

"Okay we'll give you a paper," he promised with a tinge of spite in his voice. An hour later the door opened and he threw in four newspapers. Eagerly I snatched them up and then dropped them in disappointment. They were Georgian. I could make no sense of the printed letters which looked like tiny worms writhing over the pages.

As I paced around the cell I suddenly remembered a Conan Doyle story called 'The Little Dancing Men', in which Sherlock Holmes deciphered a code made up of matchstick figures. Following his example, I resolved to make sense of those worms, yet unlike the great detective, I did not understand the language I was deciphering. The only Georgian word I knew was 'beer'. Nevertheless, I remembered that most surnames end in 'shvili', so by looking for groups of five letters I was able to work out the characters for sh, v, i and l. The paper's masthead 'Communist' was written in both Russian and Georgian, so that gave me 11 letters altogether. Pictures of Brezhnev and the cyclist Omar Pkhakadze added to my lexicon. Towards evening I was reading the paper aloud without understanding a single word. When the sergeant looked into my cell he could not believe his ears. He thought I must have been pretending not to know his language. He threw in a packet of 'Prima' cigarettes.

Reading helped pull me through my hangover. The guards told me the odd word of Georgian which I memorised as I was not allowed pen or paper. Unfortunately my solitude soon ended. My cell filled with tramps and their endless discussions about where they had drunk and how much, what the women had been like and who had beaten the shit out of whom.

A few days later, while we were exercising in the yard, I saw an old man sitting by the wall. He looked familiar somehow. I went over and—oh Lord—it was Igor Alexandrovich. He had aged considerably and resembled a decrepit old lion whose shaggy black mane was grey at the roots where filth had not yet penetrated. Igor Alexandrovich screwed up his eyes and regarded me for a long time. Then he said: "Ivan Andreyevich! Is it you?"

"The very same."

"Have you been here for a long time?"

"I'll be out in a week."

"Which cell are you in?"

"Six."

"Would you be so kind as to take me in? Do you have enough room?"

"We'll make some."

Igor Alexandrovich jumped up and came over to me. Bending his head close to mine he whispered: "Do you have lice in there?"

"Not until now," I replied, catching sight of a huge louse on his coat lapel. I pointed to it. Despite his poor sight, Igor Alexandrovich swiftly caught his household pet and for some reason dropped it into his pocket. Then our exercise period ended and we were locked up again.

A tramp in my cell said that for the last few months he had seen Igor Alexandrovich begging in the subway near the 'Collective Farmer' cinema. "When he has enough money he runs to the chemists for eau de Cologne, which he drinks from the bottle right there in the shop. When he gets too cold and tired in the subway he goes to the 'Collective Farmer'. The cashier usually lets him in without paying. He sleeps through the double bill of Indian films, warms up a bit and then returns to his pitch in the subway. At night he dosses in a basement in Chelyuskintsev Street."

They brought Igor Alexandrovich into our cell in the evening, after they had sheared his mane and treated him to a half-hearted disinfection process. To keep him at a distance we put him to sleep on a separate bunk which we called the thieves' bed. Igor Alexandrovich took this as a mark of special respect.

That evening he entertained the whole cell with a monologue on Rasputin. Believing Rasputin to have been the lover of Catherine the Great, the others listened agog, hoping to hear some dirty stories. Growing animated, Igor Alexandrovich strode up and down the cell, gesticulating wildly. Suddenly he stopped in the middle of a word, an inhuman cry came from deep inside him and he crashed to the floor in a fit. White foam bubbled from the corners of his mouth. We rushed to help him, trying to make sure he did not bite his tongue. I had seen alcoholic epilepsy before in people who stopped drinking too suddenly. We banged on the door, calling for a doctor, but the nurse had already gone home and the guards could not be bothered to ring for an ambulance.

Gradually Igor Alexandrovich's trembling ceased and he fell asleep, snoring loudly through his nose. We lifted him onto his bed. We were all frightened. Perhaps every one of us thought to himself, 'does not that fate also await me?'

When Igor Alexandrovich awoke he could remember nothing. He rose and paced about the cell. We were all silent. His head trembled and he seemed to have lost his memory. He came up to me: "Could you tell me the time please?"

"I left my watch at home on the piano."

"Yes, yes, it is easily done," he nodded. "And may I ask what your name is, if that is not confidential?"

"Pushkin, Alexander Sergeyevich," I replied.

Igor Alexandrovich knocked at the cell door asking to be let out. When the sergeant came he asked, "Would you be so kind as to tell me where I am?"

"Up your arse," replied the sergeant and went off to lie down again.

After a few hours Igor Alexandrovich recovered his senses. I told him about his fit. He sat on his bed, lost in thought for a long time. Then he looked at me with tears in his eyes: "Finita la comedia," he said.

As a doctor he understood very well what had happened and knew his end was near. "Ivan Andreyevich," he whispered to me, "I pray that death may come sooner rather than later. I would like to be done with this life."

The next day Igor Alexandrovich had another fit, an even more violent one. We all made a terrible racket but still they refused to call an ambulance. After all, it wasn't worth going through the trouble over an old beggar.

I did not see Igor Alexandrovich die, for I was released the following day and I took the first train out of Tblisi.

I went west to the town of Zestafoni, joining a group of tramps who slept under a carwash by the fruit market. Hot water pipes kept us warm in winter. When the bazaar opened in the morning I would earn a few roubles helping farmers carry goods to their stalls.

Most traders sold chacha under the counter. The police took their cut and turned a blind eye. Real chacha was a liquor distilled from grapeskins, but this was only for personal consumption. The bazaar variety was made from rotten fruit and anything that would ferment. Some brewers fortified their chacha with luminal and calcium carbide.

Near the entrance to the bazaar there were a couple of kiosks which sold odds and ends: envelopes, cosmetics and shoe laces. They were owned by two Georgians, Archil and Soso. One evening, as we sat outside the car wash, Archil came up with a three-litre barrel of chacha. He made an offer: "I'll give you this barrel if you pick up Soso's kiosk during the night and move it further away from the bazaar entrance."

"What about the cops?"

"I'll take care of them. You're not breaking into the kiosk."

"Okay."

We found an old telegraph pole, chopped it into rollers, and at night moved Soso's kiosk about 100 metres away from the entrance to the bazaar.

The next day Soso approached us, offering another barrel if we would roll his kiosk back and drag Archil's away. This went on for about two weeks. There was no real rivalry between the two men; they were simply having a joke with each other. They had a sea of chacha and they thought up this game out of boredom. Everyone has to find a way of entertaining himself.

There was a tramp in our circle who went by the name of Lousy Vassya. Lousy Vassya had lived in Zestafoni for years. Everyone knew him; some even pitied him. All year round he wrapped himself in a dirty woollen coat which had not a single button. He liked to sit in the sun scratching himself. A tall and sturdy peasant, he was swollen from constant drunkenness. Unable to do any form of work, he survived by selling his lice. From time to time a woman would approach Vassya and surreptitiously hold out a small medicine bottle. Reaching deep under his armpits, he would catch a few lice and offer them to the woman at a rouble a piece. His price was as stable as the London stock exchange. Georgian folk medicine recommended live lice as a cure for jaundice. They were mixed into yoghurt and fed unnoticed to the patient.

Tramps regarded Zestafoni as their capital, perhaps because the local police were lenient and no one had ever been jailed for vagrancy in that town. One May Day we even joined the holiday procession. A few days before, the bazaar director Vakho came to us and said, "If you go on the First of May demonstration I'll give you a barrel of wine."

This was tempting, so we got down to business. We found a couple of poles and Vakho gave us three metres of red linen. We boiled glue on our bonfire and mixed it with chalk to make paint. Then we tried to decide on a slogan. I proposed *Lenin is with us!* but the others rejected that as too inflammatory. *Peace to the World!* was too innocuous. Finally we agreed on *Zestafoni tramps salute the First of May!*

Neatly stencilling the slogan, we hid the banner under the carwash and went around the other places in town where tramps congregated. Most of them slept outside the metal plant where waste pig iron was dumped. These tramps were distinguished by their burn scars and blackened clothing. Some agreed to join us on our parade.

The parade began with schoolchildren, followed by workers from the metal plant and then other factories and institutions. We infiltrated the contingent of shop-workers, waiting till we were about 40 metres from the platform of dignitaries before falling into a group. The police did not have time to seize us and pull us out.

The bigwigs on the platform knew the order of the march so they could shout appropriate slogans to each section.

"We greet the first of May with the highest respect for study!" they cried to the schoolkids.

"Hoorah!" responded the schoolkids, probably wondering how long the farce would go on.

"The world's youth are the vanguard of Communism!" they shouted to the students.

"Hoorah!" cried the students, with even less enthusiasm.

"More goods! Cheaper and better!" they shouted to the bazaar traders.

"Hoorah!" came a half-hearted response, which translated as, 'for God's sake let's hope not, otherwise how are we going to survive?'

"A healthy mind in a healthy body!" they called to us, for according to their programme we should have been doctors.

"Hoorah!" we roared, unfurling our banner. The loudest of all was Lousy Vassya. Pulling a hand out of his armpit he waved cheerfully at the town's fathers. We could see them whispering to each other with smiles stuck on their faces. I thought to myself, 'we won't see that barrel of wine', but I was wrong. The barrel appeared that evening and we didn't need telling what to do with it.

A few days later the police came to question us. Fortunately they only laughed and decided to pretend nothing had happened. It would have been too embarrassing to take us to court.

Not long after the parade Lousy Vassya died from alcohol poisoning. He had overheard two Georgians arguing over whether anyone could drink a litre of chacha straight down. Vassya volunteered to try. He had been drunk since the morning and wanted to show off. He tipped the bottle to his lips and swallowed the chacha in great gulps. He just managed to draw the back of his hand across his mouth before he fell to the ground, black in the face. By the time someone had called an ambulance, he was dead.

Vakho and many bazaar traders donated money to bury Vassya. We held such a wake that it was a wonder no one else followed Vassya to the next world.

chapter eleven

I arrived in Tblisi on New Year's Day. I had grown bored of Zestafoni and decided to try my luck in the capital. 'Perhaps I'll cut down on my drinking, clean up and find some sort of permanent job,' I thought. This time I knew better than to hang around the station, so I took a trolleybus into town. I usually avoided public transport, for you could never get your bearings through the filthy windows. I preferred to walk the streets of a strange city to orientate myself, but I was tired that morning, and in urgent need of a hair-of-the-dog.

In the town centre I stopped at a beer stall. It was crowded and I had to look around for some elbow space. Suddenly a gravel voice called out: "Over here mate!"

I went across to three men, alkashi by the look of them. The one who had hailed me sported a pair of broken glasses and a pointed beard. "Where are you from?" he asked.

"From where the wind blows."

"And where do you stay?"

"Where the night finds me."

"And what do they call you?"

"Ivan."

"Ivan the what?"

"Simply Ivan—that's my name."

"Nothing in this world is simple; not even a boil can lance itself. I know Ivan Moneybags and Ivan the Terrible... Which one are you?"

"None. I am from Chapaevsk."

"Let me see... the Terrible was the Fourth so that makes you Ivan the Fifth."

He held out his hand: "Kalinin."

"Kalinin who?"

"Kalinin the Chairman of the Supreme Soviet!" he laughed. "Now we must drink to this meeting!"

Everyone rummaged in their pockets. I offered a rouble but Kalinin put out his hand to stop me.

"Today you are our guest!"

One of my new friends ran across the road to a wine shop and returned with a bottle of champagne. I was disappointed, but Kalinin gave me a sly wink and approached another table where several well-dressed

Georgians were gathered. Politely, he wished them a Happy New Year and offered them the champagne. Then he returned to our table. In a few minutes the Georgians had sent over two bottles of champagne, a half-litre of vodka, and a dozen beers. We plunged into the beer and vodka. After a while we sent the two bottles of champagne over to another group of Georgians. In an hour there were so many bottles on our table there was not even room to rest our elbows.

Kalinin, a former physics teacher, lived by begging. He really did look like the former Chairman of the Supreme Soviet of the USSR, and he shrewdly exploited this resemblance.

"When I strike my pose on the Elbakidze bridge people stop and stare. Then they feel they have to throw me a coin. You can find me on the bridge at any time; the police leave me alone so long as I keep quiet. The trouble is, after I've had a few the urge comes over me to deliver a speech. My oratorical talent has landed me in the spets a few times."

That night Kalinin showed me a place to sleep. Under one of Tblisi's parks there was a cavern housing steam pipes that heated the city. In winter every railway prostitute, professional beggar, bazaar cock sucker, tramp and thief drifted to that cavern. Some were so weakened by illness and drinking that they hardly ever left the place. Others went about their business by day and gathered again in the evening, bringing food and drink. All night long the cavern seethed with songs, curses and fights.

It was a murky place, lit only by candles stolen by church beggars. Rats scurried over the bodies of sleeping tramps. The floor was covered in crusts of bread, slimy pieces of rotting liver sausage and shattered eau de Cologne bottles. Wine and vodka empties were collected up early in the morning. We slept on cardboard thrown out of furniture stores. Every few days one of the sick cavern dwellers died, or occasionally someone was killed in a knife fight. When there was a death we all left the cavern, somebody tipped off the police and we made ourselves scarce while they came to collect the body.

Hippies had made their appearance in Georgia by that time and some of them tried to join us. We despised them as dilettantes and kicked them out of the cavern whenever they hung around for too long. Once in a while, however, some Tblisi artist or intellectual would decide he wanted to experience life in the lower depths—and offer to pay for the privilege. Then we put on a real feast with songs and folk dances. We tramps knew perfectly well what was expected of us and earned the bottles that our visitors brought. Putting our arms around our free-spirited friends, we spun endless yarns about our lives, sparing no harrowing detail.

The bacchanalia usually ended in a police raid. Nervous about entering our cavern, the cops sent in dogs first, and sometimes flushed us out with CS gas. Emerging tramps were thrown into waiting Black Marias. I was caught in one of these round-ups but managed to slip away in the confusion. I spent the rest of the night in the park and thereafter tried to avoid the cavern.

The morning after the raid found me wandering aimlessly down Plekhanov Avenue, as hungry as a wolf pack in winter. My brains splashed about somewhere in the depths of my skull; the rest of my head was a barrel of pain and grief. The sudden hoot of a car made me break into a cold sweat. I felt that people on the other side of the street were watching me and whispering vicious words of condemnation. I had no money. I had already been around the beer stalls and met not a single acquaintance. It seemed that in an hour I would breathe my last, yet I was too scared to ask a stranger for a few kopecks. Keeping close to the wall I slunk along with my eyes to the ground.

"Have you lost something?" I suddenly heard a voice above my head. A tall beggar stood with his back to the wall, propped up on two crutches.

"A purse—except I didn't lose it; I'm hoping to find it."

"No one has lost anything here today, that's for sure. I've been here since morning."

"Too bad," I said, moving off.

"Stop!" he cried. "Can you help me?"

"How?"

"I need to buy a bottle but it's hard for me to get to the shop."

"But my pockets are empty."

"I've got the cash. I'll wait for you on that little square over there."

"Okay."

"My hangover is killing me," he sighed.

"Mine too."

He poured a pile of change into my hand.

"There's more than enough for a bottle here," I said.

"Buy two so you won't waste time running back to the shop later."

When I came out of the shop I saw my saviour moving slowly towards the square, thrusting his crutches forward and dragging his body in their wake. He was paralysed from his shoulders down. I joined him and we introduced ourselves. His name was Borya and he came from Leningrad.

I discovered that Borya was no drinker and had only sent me for the wine because he had guessed the state I was in. He drank a glass to be sociable but refused a refill.

"I've been paralysed since I was a student. I jumped from a train to avoid the ticket collector. If he had reported me for travelling without a ticket the college would have cut off my grant. I had no family to support me. Since then I've been all over Russia. Once in a while the police pick me up and send me to an invalid home, but I always run away. I arrive in some town or other and don't leave it until I have collected 1000 roubles."

"And then?" I asked.

"I bury them and go on to another town."

"Are you trying to save a lot of money—to retire perhaps?"

"No. I don't need the money itself. I give most of it away."

"But why do you live like this? You stand the whole day long at your pitch, collecting money. You don't drink, you don't smoke and you give it all away?"

"The money is not the most important thing. I make people happy."

"How?"

"Imagine; I am standing on my pitch, virtually a corpse. A man goes by. I don't know anything about him. Perhaps he is a cruel person who beat his wife that morning. I have never seen him before and I shall probably never see him again. He notices me, fumbles in his pocket, finds a three-kopeck piece that is no use to him and chucks it into my cap. To me those three kopecks are nothing, but I have done something for that man."

"What have you done?"

"I have caused him to do good. When he passes on down the road he is a different person, although he may not even know it himself. Even if he gave me the money automatically, without thinking, he has become a slightly better person all the same."

I looked at Borya as stunned as a bull in a slaughterhouse. He laughed. "I can see that you are not yourself yet. Here is some more money. I am going to work. Meet me in Gorky Park this evening?"

"Agreed."

Borya poured some change into my hand, then he stood up. Swaying his body like a pendulum, he went back to his pitch.

I was anxious to continue our conversation, so I did as Borya suggested and made for the park. As I neared his pitch I crossed to the other side of the street to pass unnoticed in the throng of pedestrians. The sight of me might have reminded Borya of his kindness; I sensed he was not in need of my gratitude.

Picking up a bottle of Imereti wine along the way, I chose a far bench in the park where I could sit hidden behind some bushes. From time to time I took a slug of wine, trying to maintain myself on that blissful cusp between sobriety and drunkenness.

Long-supressed thoughts bubbled up in my mind: 'Who am I? An alcoholic and a tramp. But I am no white raven; half the country are alcoholics. Our alcoholics outnumber the populations of France and Spain combined. And that's only the men. If you count women too you have to add all Scandinavia and throw in Monaco for good measure.

'Unlike me, however, most people work, or at least give the impression that they are working. And for what? Just to drink away their pay at the end of the month. Many men claim they work for the sake of their family. But what's the good of an alcoholic in a family? Do the empties buy babies' milk? I've seen children tremble at the sound of their fathers' footsteps. At least I had the honesty to ditch the pretence and become a tramp, although it cost me my wife and daughter.

'The worst thing you can do to someone else is humiliate them, but self-degradation is no less evil. The person who humiliates himself drags others down with him. I have seen this happen often enough and I don't want to be guilty of it too. Yes, I made the right decision back in that forest in the Kuban. I am responsible only to myself now. So the one question remains: how am I going to live? I won't steal, and it's hard to find work, so how will I buy my drink? In practice I am almost a beggar, although I try not to admit this. I lie to myself and shut my eyes to the truth. But when all is said and done I have to recognise what I am.

'Why am I not ashamed to accept Borya's money while I won't hold out my own hand in the street? I don't consider myself better than him. It's not the first time a beggar has bought me a drink. I can't bring myself to beg, yet I drink at someone else's expense, and that is the same thing.'

Another part of my consciousness interrupted: 'But beggars also live at others' expense.

'No,' I corrected myself, 'beggars support themselves. They earn their kopecks through self-abasement.'

All the same I was mistrustful of beggars. I had known hundreds: on the streets, in camps, police cells and psychiatric institutions. Most of them were scoundrels and hypocrites. Many times I had heard them ask a passer-by, "Give me a few kopecks for the love of God."

When the person passed on they would say, "May you rot in hell you greedy bastard!"

I sometimes asked them, "How can you talk like that? It's up to them whether they give to you or not. Besides that, other people might overhear and what would they think of you then?"

"Fuck them. They are many and I am only one. If one passes by another will drop something in my cap. Only God sees everything!"

But it was not for me to sit in judgement. Everyone lived as they could.

In former times whole villages had worked as beggars, training their children to follow the family profession. These beggars roamed the countryside, pretending to have lost all their wordly goods in a fire. Others hung around stations asking for the price of a ticket, saying all their money and documents had been stolen. In Astrakhan camp I had met a man who had spent years selling a saw outside Moscow stations. He worked with great artistry, dividing his time between Moscow's eleven termini. His victims were officers: none below the rank of major. He would go up to the officer, salute, stand at attention and bark: "Comrade Colonel! May I introduce myself? Sergeant-Major Sidorov, of the 187th Standard Bearers, guards division, Order of Suvorov!"

"What can I do for you, Sergeant-Major?"

"Excuse me, Comrade Colonel! Would you buy my saw?" Sidorov brought out a wrapped-up saw from behind his back.

"But why should I buy your saw, Sergeant-Major?"

"I want to rejoin my family but I need 23 roubles for the ticket. I'll sell you the saw for five."

"Haven't you been to the Commandant's office?"

"Of course, Comrade Colonel, but as everyone knows, they are just a bunch of pen-pushers. They've never smelled gunpowder. I remember, now, near Breslau . . ."

At this point the colonel usually pulled out his wallet and gave Sidorov a 25 rouble bill. If the officer was at all suspicious he might ask: "Who was the commander at your Front?"

"Marshall Zhukov, Comrade Colonel!" replied Sidorov with shining eyes. "Now there was a true officer! He loved his men." Sidorov had learned the history of the 187th Standard Bearers off by heart. If the officer asked any tricky questions Sidorov would reply, "I don't remember. I was in hospital at the time, wounded in action."

Sidorov continued to offer his saw for six years. In the end people got to know him and he grew careless, accosting officers when he was already drunk. Finally he was arrested and sent to camp. He was a born actor and the way I saw it he earned his drinks.

Like Sidorov and Kalinin, plenty of beggars earned their money through guile, but most played on pity; it was simpler and yielded good results. I knew that almost every human being was capable of feeling pity—perhaps even Cannibal of Ashkhabad camp—but I could not bring myself to exploit this feeling.

I had to admit, though, that I often earned my drinks through wit. Every intelligent drinker tries to be charming, even when he is not inclined to be. It's his survival mechanism. I survived by making people laugh. In a way my crippled leg helped, because no one felt threatened by me.

Yet there is a difference between singing for your supper and holding out your hand for it. I feared begging as a way of life. It might be too easy. Once I had weighed anchor outside some church or bazaar I would probably never return to a normal existence. And I still entertained hopes in that direction. Hopes are the last to die and I clutched at them, sustained by memories of the past.

That evening was dark and rainy. When Borya arrived he and I took shelter in a half-constructed building near the park. I gathered some rubbish and made a small bonfire. We spread newspapers on the cement floor and sat talking. I got completely pissed but Borya drank nothing. He had tied a hot-water bottle to his thigh and urine trickled into it almost constantly. This embarrassed him so he tried not to drink, even refusing water.

Borya told me more about his life: "Once I went to a public library in Leningrad to try to read something on begging, but I was disappointed. No one writes the truth. They slide over the surface of the question. Perhaps because they never write from the point of view of the beggar. Not even Dostoevsky. As for Tolstoy, he was a great sham. He went out punctually every day to give alms but before he would part with a kopeck he took away the beggar's very soul with his nosy questioning.

"The truth is, when I beg I inspire pity, and pity is always a blessing, no matter how dirty the soul in which it springs," Borya concluded.

"I cannot agree with you," I said. "Pity is a good and natural emotion, but do you remember Yesenin's lines: *arousing tears in my heart is like throwing stones at the glass of my watch?* Only a wretch would deliberately try to awaken a person's compassion. It a cheap thing to do."

Yet I could not criticise Borya for I realised that my way of life was essentially no different to his. The only distinction between us was that I did not see myself as a person who did good to others. Anyone who does good becomes a slightly better person himself, but if you plan in advance to do good then the deed loses all its grace. If I did good, then let it be by accident. Most likely I did no good at all in this world, and I certainly would not do so by begging.

Our divergent views sprang from a more fundamental difference. "Borya," I observed, "you believe in God, but I do not. If there was a God there would be justice, and as there is none in this world, so there can be no God."

Borya objected: "But you can't judge God by your

own standards of right and wrong. It is impossible to comprehend God. You simply have to believe."

"I can't 'simply believe' when life is so unfair. Why was I born here, now, in a country where it makes no difference which side of the barbed wire you are on? Why did you fall under a train?"

"Marcus Aurelius said, almost 20 centuries ago, 'Humanity does not yet have the wisdom to test whether there is justice or not.'"

"Well, that was 2,000 years ago."

"That only proves his point—the time has not yet come."

Borya and I arranged to meet the following evening but we missed each other and I never saw him again.

The next day I boarded the No. 5 tram on Klara Zetkin street. A man offered me his seat but I shook my head. When the tram moved I took off my beret and turned to the passengers.

"Good health and good luck!
Live as well as your pay permits,
and if you can't survive on it,
Well, then, don't. No one is forcing you!"

As I finished my verse the passengers burst out laughing. The words struck home, because no one could afford to live on their pay, not even the police. A woman held out a 20 kopeck piece and asked, "You'll be getting yourself a beer with that, I suppose?"

"Not only beer but vodka too!"

She put the coin back in her purse, found a rouble and gave it to me. When I had worked the whole tram

I got off, boarded the next one and repeated the performance. By the time I reached Collective Farm Square I had nearly 20 roubles. Some people grumbled that I was just collecting money for my hair-of-the-dog, but I was not offended. It was up to them whether they gave or not. I was not greedy. Having collected a little money I threw in the towel, bought a bottle and continued to drink throughout the day, inviting anyone who wished to join me. I had no shortage of companions.

The next day I went to work again, and the next until it became a way of life that I no longer stopped to consider. The police caught me a couple of times, but they either laughed at my verses or threw me off the tram.

Begging was not always as easy as it had been that first day. Sometimes the trams were so packed I could not move among the passengers; sometimes they were too empty to be worth boarding. It rained for nearly three weeks. I froze and fell ill. For a while I slept at the top of a lift shaft in an eight-storey block of flats. I would crawl up after midnight, but I was eventually discovered by a resident who threatened to call the police. My clothes became filthy and ragged, my shoes split, and I never had enough money for a new pair. I grew desperately tired of spending the whole day on my feet. I longed for a good night's sleep but the cops drove me out of the railway station and it was impossible to take a nap on the short Tblisi underground. The bathhouse was a godsend, allowing me to reheat my bones, but I could not linger for too long or they might have thrown me out and barred me from future visits. When I was absolutely dropping from fatigue I would slip five roubles to a train conductor and take an overnight trip.

I'd stretch out along a seat and enjoy five or six hours of deep, refreshing sleep, not caring whether the train took me to Baku or Yerevan.

At night I would open a bottle to see me through till morning. As I swallowed my wine I was sometimes struck by guilt over the way I had earned it. 'Don't judge yourself so harshly,' I thought, 'what choice do you have?' But I knew I was just making excuses. The cycle of self-recrimination spun round my head as I tried to fall asleep. 'What are you living for?' I wondered.

Although I was drinking a lot, alcohol was having less effect on me. Soon I needed two or three bottles of fortified wine just to see me through the night, otherwise I could not even drop off for half an hour. When sleep came it was crowded with nightmares that left me exhausted.

There was a slope between the road and the river where townspeople came to tip their rubbish. In this place of unimaginable filth I could sometimes find unbroken bottles. The wine shop would exchange these for a bottle of Rkatseli.

At the top of the slope there was a small overhang. It gave me shelter and I was unseen from the road. Here I huddled at night. The rubbish below me reeked of rotten meat and excrement, but I was scarcely bothered by the smell. I would lean back against the earth, half-propped up, with an open bottle between my legs, smoking and taking a swig of wine as soon as I started to feel bad. For months I had derived no pleasure at all from alcohol, but I needed it to ward off the d.ts.

When I had emptied my bottle I would drag myself

out of my lair and limp down to Klara Zetkin street. There, in a courtyard behind a little gate, was the 'fountain of life', open 24 hours a day for the suffering and the greedy. When I opened the gate the house-dogs barely stirred, so used were they to night-time callers. I stumbled through the courtyard and up a couple of steps to a verandah. Inside the verandah was a table with a three-litre jar of chacha standing on it. Beside it was a cut-glass tumbler and a plate of bread and spring onion. An old woman slept on a huge bed beside the table—or at least she gave the impression of sleeping.

I laid my coins on the table. They were sweaty and crusted with tobacco. A withered hand shot out from the bed, grabbed the coins and stuffed them somewhere among a heap of rags. Having drunk my glass I slunk out of the courtyard, shaking and trying not to throw up.

The devil only knows what those Georgians mixed with their chacha. I broke out in large boils like soft corns which itched and stung. I tried not to squeeze them as I knew that would make them worse, but when a boil the size of a walnut grew on my heel I had to burst it before I could get my shoe on. By the end of the day I could hardly walk for the pain. There were no bandages in the chemist. I went to Mikhailovski hospital but they threw me out because of the disgusting state I was in. Finally the blood donor clinic where I had occasionally earned a few roubles gave me a bandage. I rinsed the wound under a tap in the street and bound up my foot.

After that I felt better and I was able to do a little work on the No. 5 tram. I was not collecting much money these days, probably because I smelled so bad that people turned their heads at my approach.

In the morning I gritted my teeth as I tore the bandage off my raw skin. I rinsed it under a courtyard tap but could not wait for it to dry as I had to get to work. The damp material picked up dust and filth from the street as I walked. By dusk the wound was itching unbearably; but I took that as a sign that it was healing. However, a few nights later I unwound the bandage to find a mass of white worms writhing in the open flesh. I did not panic. 'It will only be a matter of time before gangrene sets in,' I thought. I was in some sort of stupor; it was as if the foot belonged to someone else. All the same I carefully rinsed it and bound it up again.

That night on the rubbish dump I settled down with two bottles of Rkatseli to keep me going till dawn. I propped myself up against the bank, dropping off for a couple of minutes, waking with a start and swallowing a couple of mouthfuls of wine. I kept a strict watch over the level of liquid in the bottle, telling myself: 'hold on, hold on, it's not evening yet!' Reflecting on my situation I laughed out loud: 'Look at you, my boy!' I even mumbled a verse that came into my head:

"My room—a stinking garbage pit
My bed—an old newspaper
More than one tramp died here
And so it seems, shall I"

I did not know whether I would live till dawn, but I did not care too much either way. 'Let death come tonight,' I thought. 'It will put an end to life's torments once and for all.' But I did fear the d.ts. I feared I would lose control and do something very bad. And I was deeply ashamed of my filthy, festering body. I had not been to the bathhouse for weeks; my wound prevented me from using the communal pool and I could not afford a private cabin. I was filled with shame as I imagined the state my body would be in when it was found in the morning.

But I did not die on that Tblisi rubbish dump. In the morning I managed to drag myself out of my lair, gather some empties and limp over to the liquor store. I came out of the shop clutching a litre of fortified wine in each hand. As I crossed Mardzhanishvili Square I tripped and fell, instinctively flinging up my arms to save the bottles. My face slammed into the asphalt and my forehead cracked open, but by some miracle the bottles remained intact. I groaned with relief and passed out.

I awoke to find myself lying on the pavement with a crowd gathered about me.

"We've called an ambulance," a voice said.

Realising the police would not be involved, I relaxed and let myself be carried off to hospital. I did not care that my nose was broken and my eyes so swollen I could barely see; I feared only the d.ts, which were fast approaching. Believing that I had been witness to a dreadful crime and the police wanted to interview me, I tried to hide. I was also convinced that the perpetrator of the crime was tracking me down in order to kill me. In mortal terror of every living soul, I leaped out of bed and ran around the hospital, squeezing into dark cupboards and cowering under beds.

The staff finally caught me, put me in a strait jacket and packed me off to 'Happy Village', a large psychiatric institution in the mountains. There I was cared for by an unusually kind young doctor who paid no attention to my repulsive appearance. She even suggested I go to a special clinic to have my nose repaired but I declined: "I'm not intending to star in any film; I need a psychiatrist not a surgeon."

The doctor ordered me to be tied to a bed and then she injected me with Sulfazine[1]. With diabolic strength I tore off the sheets that bound me and ran away. Although the staff had removed the handles of the ward doors I managed to prise them open with a dinner spoon. I ran out of the hospital and down the road. I was caught two blocks from the clinic, dragged back, tied up again and given another shot of Sulfazine. My temperature soared. For two or three days I lay motionless, soaked in sweat. Gradually I returned to my senses. When I admitted to the doctor that no one wanted to kill me she took me off Sulfazine and ordered me to be untied.

Soon I was cracking jokes with the doctor and making her laugh. Through her contacts she found me a job as a nightwatchman in a Tblisi theatre. With a roof over my head I was able to keep off the drink for several months. One day, however, I ran into Tolik, an old friend from Zestafoni who was trying his luck begging in the capital. He had nowhere to sleep. I could not recommend the cavern so we arranged that when the theatre performance ended Tolik would tap on my

---

[1] Sulfazine is a powerful tranquillizer.

window and I would let him in for the night. He slept curled up on some newspaper in a corner, refusing my offer of the couch: "No, no, Vanya, I wet myself after I've had a bottle or two."

Despite his alcoholism Tolik was so sharp he only had to look at a few lines of Pravda to arrive at conclusions we would hear a month later on Voice of America. He told me that something was changing in the USSR. "But what difference will it make to our lives, Tolik?" I asked. "What happens in Moscow might as well take place on the moon."

The theatre management knew about my weakness and tried to keep me away from the bottle. However it seemed churlish not to accompany Tolik when he poured his wine at night. Early in the morning he would sneak out, taking the empties with him. He spent the day begging and I gave him some money from my pay to buy bottles for the night.

It was not long, however, before we overdid things. The director arrived one morning to find me sitting among the scenery as drunk as wine itself. Tolik stood in the centre of the stage, striking the pose of a Roman senator as he declaimed Bezimensky's 'Tragedian Night'. All around us rolled empty bottles. We were puffing away like the Battleship Potemkin, although smoking was strictly forbidden in the theatre. They drove my friend away and called an ambulance for me. I was taken back to Happy Village and this time the doctor was less kind.

I had been away from Chapaevsk for many years and hardly kept in touch with my family, apart from the occasional phone call to my sister. After my second cure I received news from her that our mother had died. I returned to Chapaevsk for the last time, staying with my sister and her family. I did not understand them nor they me, but we were civil to each other.

My sister was the only family member I had left in Chapaevsk. Dobrinin had died some years before. Uncle Volodya had moved to the Ukraine. After he became a widower I heard he took to drink. My wife and daughter had been living in Estonia since they left me back in 1967. I heard news of them occasionally via my sister.

I wondered whether I should try to find out what had happened to my real father. Since the time of Khrushchev I had accepted that he had been shot. In the new climate of political openness it might have been possible to learn details of his arrest and trial. 'No,' I thought, 'it might be better if I did not know the truth. If he was a Chekist he was probably responsible for sending people to their deaths.'

My sister said there was some furniture left from our parents' house that she would like to sell.

"Keep the money," I told her, "all I want is enough for a ticket out of this hell-hole."

"Where are you going?"

"Who knows? Fiji maybe."

And I really was thinking how good it would be to leave the country. Preferably forever.

Just before I left Chapaevsk I ran into a couple of old drinking acquaintances who were returning unsteadily from the cemetery. "Poor old thing," they said, after exchanging greetings with me, "They let us join the wake so it would look as though she had someone to mourn her. We only knew her by sight; she died in the old people's home."

"Who was it?"

"Marussya Timofeyevna. Perhaps you knew her. She used to live in Bersol."

It was our old nanny, Cyclops. I pitied her then, for her life had been even more wretched than mine. After she left my parents she had looked after children in other Party families until she became too old and infirm. Having no one to care for her, she had entered the home. It was the oldest building in town and worse than any strict regime prison. The staff stole all the food and left the inmates to decay in their own filth. As you passed the home you could see the old people standing outside on metal balconies, gazing forlornly at a world they had already left.

'That's where I would end up if I stayed here,' I thought, 'providing I did not drink myself to death first.'

epilogue
a city in the west

The details of how I came here are not important. Let us just say I jumped ship. At first I was excited by my new surroundings. Like every naive Russian visitor I marvelled at the shops. 'You could cover our walls with their toilet paper,' I wrote to my sister, 'and vodka is cheaper than eau de Cologne. Why drink substitutes when you can afford the real thing?'

I discovered that our propagandists did not lie about the decadence of the West. People go around in clothes that would shame a Zestafoni tramp and not only the poor: the other day I saw a young man walk out of an expensive restaurant in a grey Soviet prison jacket.

I remember the shock I felt the first time I saw a teenage girl drinking from a bottle in the street, although she was only drinking water. Now I am used to seeing people drink straight from the bottle. Back home we rarely stooped that low; even tramps kept personal drinking vessels. In any Russian park, if you look carefully, you will see a glass under a hedge or bush, covered over with twigs so that dirt does not fall into it. But perhaps we were more concerned with practicalities than appearances, for when your hands are shaking like death it is impossible to lift a bottle to your lips. Besides, to spill a glass is a misfortune; to spill a bottle is a tragedy.

The worst thing of all about the West is the sight of so many people turning their lives into an endless scramble for money. Most are rich beyond the dreams of a Chapaevsk citizen, yet they never seem content with what they have. This system is a treadmill, not freedom.

It is really all the same to me now whether I remain here or go back to Russia. Perhaps I only stay through inertia. I have settled into life, with my own room and a small pension. My furniture comes from the streets: chairs, mattress, sofa, vacuum cleaner, TV and a video that I repaired myself. At night I like to wander around my neighbourhood, seeing what I can pick up. Looking through people's rubbish I learn a lot about them—

what they read and what they eat, whether they are drinkers and if they are ashamed of what they drink.

From time to time new arrivals from Russia come to stay with me while they get settled. They expect the streets to be paved with gold, but they can only find illegal work in restaurants or cab driving. Some give up and go home again, tired of being treated as less than human. They remind me of myself leaving home all those years ago.

I hardly mix with local people. At my age it is hard to learn a new language. Even if I could communicate we would not understand each other. I am not lonely; on the contrary, I sometimes long to go away from this city to a quiet village by the seashore, where I shall know no one at all.

Mostly I occupy my time by thinking about my past, trying to make sense of it all. Like the disgraced teachers and engineers of Toliatti's market-place I always held the Soviet system responsible for my downfall. Throughout my life I felt plagued and persecuted by Komsomolists, bosses, judges and camp Godfathers. This is not to say that when I poured myself a glass of wine in the morning I did it as an act of protest against the system. Of course not. But it consoled me to think that if I drank too much it was because I had no choice.

Now my old line of defence has fallen away. I am free from Komsomolists and Godfathers but I still drink. At least I know that whatever I have done, however deeply I have degraded myself, I shall pay for it. The thought cheers me slightly.

Despite everything I sometimes thank God that I

became an alcoholic and took to the road. Instead of spinning out my days in Chapaevsk, talking of nothing but work and how many potatoes my allotment has yielded, I have broken through barriers that confine the normal human being. I have discovered that things I once feared hold no terrors at all. I learned that I could live without a home, possessions or human companionship.

I have not cut myself off completely from my past; I even have occasional letters from Olga. She never remarried. When my sister told her I had emigrated she started to entertain hopes, perhaps thinking I had come off the bottle at last. Well, I soon dashed those hopes; I told her that the West has given me no reason to stop drinking. Then she wrote back: Come home Vanya, let us show you how to live.

Her arrogance made me angry. After all these years she still cannot understand what led me to drink in the first place. I was not interested in becoming the ideal Soviet family man. Well, the truth is, I was just not ready for a family at all. Yet at the same time her letter aroused feelings of guilt, especially towards my daughter.

'Damn them all,' I thought after reading the letter. 'What did they expect? I should be proud of the fact that I resisted their pressure to change into someone I am not.'

I picked up my stick and set off to see if any of my drinking mates were congregated by the war memorial. It did not matter that I couldn't understand their speech; we shared a language that went deeper than words.

It was a cold, raw day. My sore kidneys twinged and the filthy air made me wheeze more than usual. As I was passing MacDonalds I caught the eye of an acquaintance through the window. I halted and he rushed to the door of the restaurant:

"Vanya!" he called. "Where are you going?"

"Hello Grisha. For a walk."

He fell in beside me. Grisha had arrived a couple of years ago with his family. He usually took great care of his appearance but this morning he was unshaven and his clothes were crumpled.

"I've left home," he said, "to teach them a lesson. My wife and her mother ganged up on me again. All I wanted was a mobile phone, for God's sake. What kind of a man am I without one? They said we couldn't afford it. I know my mother-in-law just wants to humiliate me. She doesn't respect me."

Neither did I. But I liked Grisha's mother-in-law. Some Russians say that the world is like a piece of Swiss cheese; if you take on a black hole yourself that is one less piece of evil to plague someone else. By giving Grisha a place to stay for a while I would be lifting a burden from his family's shoulders. Besides, for once I felt like some company.

"Grisha, let things calm down. You can sleep on my sofa."

"Vanya, you've saved my life," he said, clapping me on the shoulder.

I noticed we were passing a supermarket. To cheer him up I suggested: "How about a bottle?"

The next few days were a blur. I only remember waking up at the foot of my stairs with my pockets empty and my walking stick broken. My body ached as though it had been beaten by a whole station of policemen. Grabbing the bannisters, I hauled myself up to my room. After swallowing the pain killers my doctor had given me, I lay down.

That night I felt the terror return. I stared into it like a rabbit transfixed before a cobra, knowing there was no means of escape. I had to act while I could still think.

Most of my Russian acquaintances knew my habits and would no longer help me, but I remembered Irina, a young girl from Rostov, who was kinder than the others. I picked up the phone.

"Irina, I am going to die tonight for sure," I said, "Call a taxi and take me to hospital."

"Ivan Andreyevich, you know the hospital won't admit you again."

"Excuse me for troubling you."

I put the phone down just in time. The mouthpiece had started to crackle with sounds I identified as Voice of America.

Irina was right. Since being in this country I had dried out in the local hospital four times. The detox clinic wouldn't take me again either. Not that they were much use. They insisted on talking about my past, how I related to my father and similar nonsense. They expected me to bare my soul to some young kid who didn't understand me at all. I told them to give me injections, to knock me out while I got over the worst of the d.ts, but they refused. They probably thought I was a drug addict.

While in detox I drank all the mouthwash I had brought with me, but that wasn't enough. I managed to get to a phone and call Grisha, who brought in a hot water bottle full of vodka. Somehow the doctors found out I had been drinking and told me to leave. I lost my temper and raged at them but they would not relent. Well, what did they expect?

I am tired. Why should I stop drinking? There is nothing else left for me in life. I just require a little help when I've overdone things. Someone has to knock me out while the alcohol drains from my body.

Hours pass and with every minute I feel more scared. If only I could ride through this one I'd stop drinking for a while and then keep things under control, like I managed to in Georgia.

The TV flickers. Silent cues shoot coloured balls across the screen. They are not enough to distract me. Rain patters on my window. The street lamp outside my room casts a yellow pool of light on the wet pavement. Tiny devils frolic in the gutter. If I drop my guard they will climb up the drainpipe and slip in under the windowframe.

I close my eyes and wait for night. Alarms wail in the distance. Cement mixers roar up and down the road. A sharp pain jabs through my leg; I sit up in time to see a devil running across the floor, squealing and brandishing his fork. I yell and Grisha hurries out of the kitchen with a bottle in his hand. Cradling my head in his arm, he wedges a pen between my teeth, unscrews the bottle cap and puts the neck to my lips. Gratefully I let the liquid trickle onto my tongue.

some of ivan's travels

1950–51
Spitzbergen
ARCTIC OCEAN
Murmansk
Barents Sea
Kara Sea
Baltic Sea
ESTONIA
Riga
LITHUANIA
LATVIA
Arkhangelsk
Nar'ian Mar
Dvina R.
BYELARUS
Igarka
Arctic Circle
Moscow
Ural Mountains
RUSSIA
UKRAINE
Kharkov
Tambov
Kazan
Syzran
Toliatti
Kuibyshev
Chapaevsk
Volga R.
Yenisei R.
Black Sea
Kropotkin
Armavir
Astrakhan
GEORGIA
Caspian Sea
Tbilisi
KAZAKHSTAN
ARMENIA
Aral Sea
Baku
AZERBAIJAN
Krasnovodsk
UZBEKISTAN
Chimkent
TURKMENISTAN
Tashkent
KYRGYZSTAN
Ashkhabad
Ferçana
0
500 Miles
TAJKISTAN
Tien Shan
CHINA
AFGHANISTAN

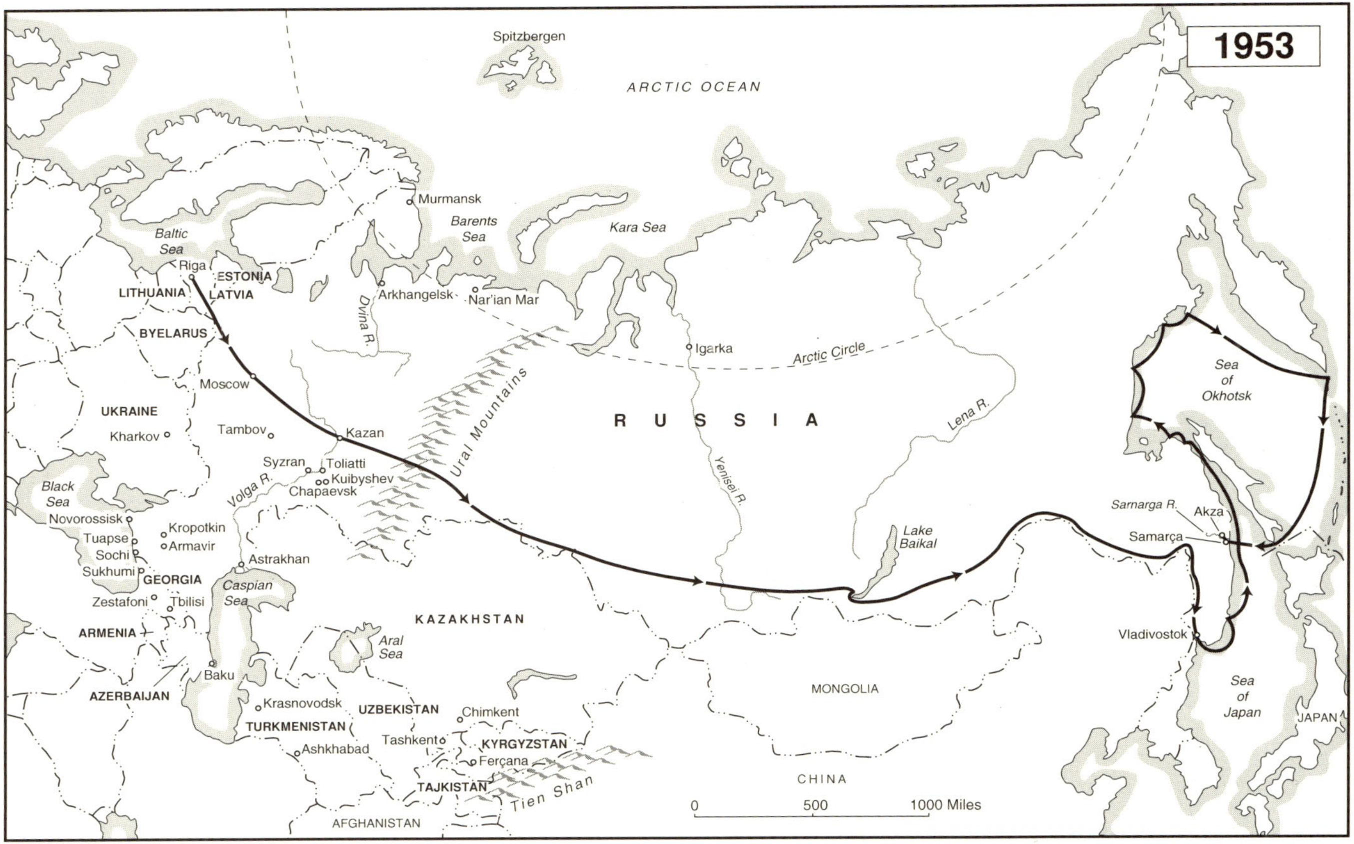
1953
Spitzbergen
ARCTIC OCEAN
Murmansk
Barents Sea
Kara Sea
Baltic Sea
Riga
ESTONIA
LATVIA
LITHUANIA
Arkhangelsk
Nar'ian Mar
Dvina R.
BYELARUS
Igarka
Arctic Circle
Moscow
Ural Mountains
UKRAINE
R U S S I A
Lena R.
Sea of Okhotsk
Tambov
Kharkov
Kazan
Syzran
Toliatti
Kuibyshev
Chapaevsk
Volga R.
Black Sea
Yenisei R.
Novorossisk
Kropotkin
Armavir
Tuapse
Sochi
Sukhumi
GEORGIA
Astrakhan
Caspian Sea
Zestafoni
Tbilisi
ARMENIA
Lake Baikal
Samarga R.
Akza
Samarça
KAZAKHSTAN
Aral Sea
Baku
AZERBAIJAN
Krasnovodsk
UZBEKISTAN
Chimkent
TURKMENISTAN
Tashkent
KYRGYZSTAN
Ashkhabad
Ferçana
TAJKISTAN
Tien Shan
AFGHANISTAN
MONGOLIA
CHINA
0
500
1000 Miles
Vladivostok
Sea of Japan
JAPAN

1968

1971–72

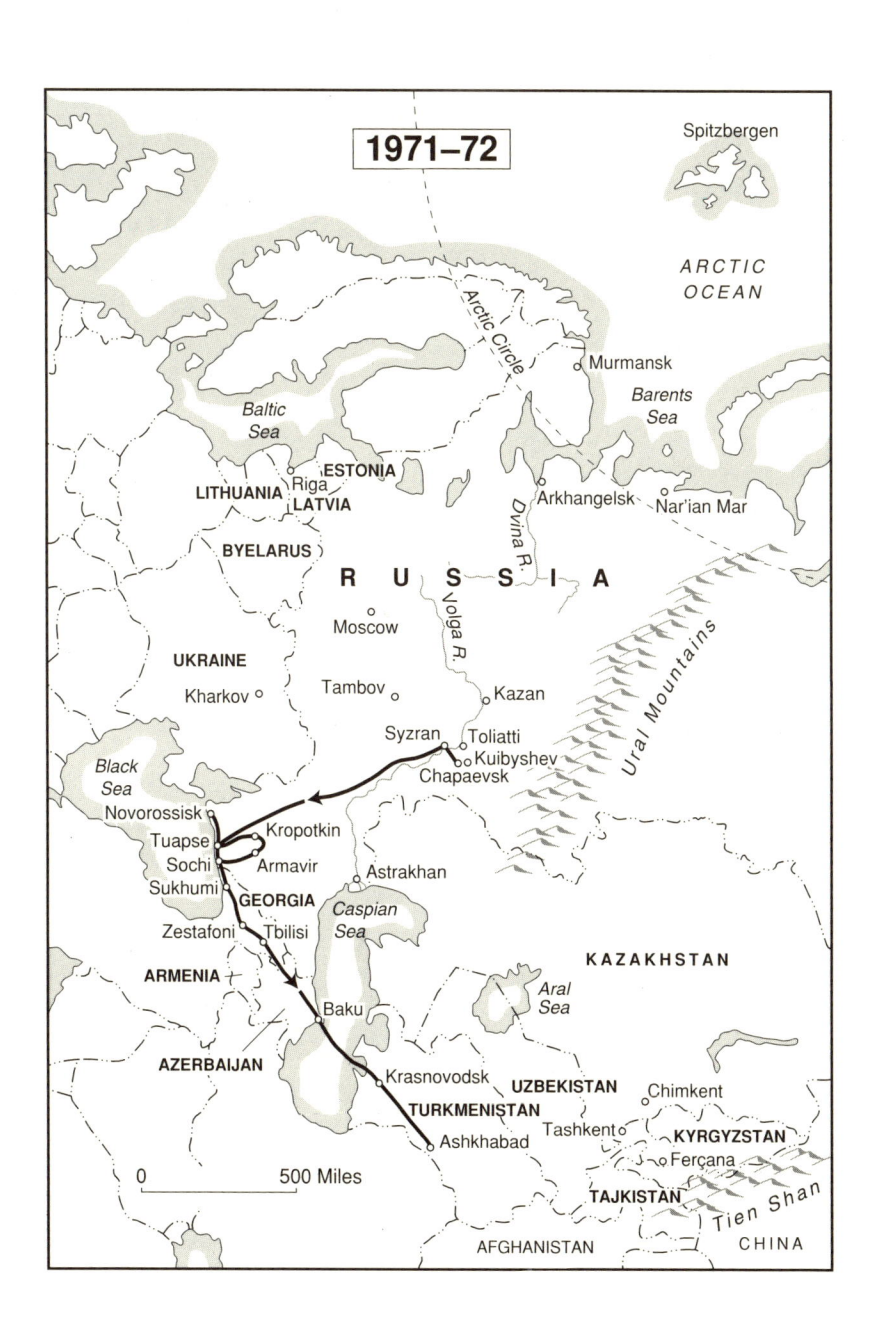

acknowledgements

I am grateful to the following for their help and advice: Jeff Kelly, Ross Morley, Helen O'Connor, Helen O'Donovan, Carol Taylor, Catherine and John Walton, Joley Wood and Martin Wright. Above all, I want to thank Ivan for his kindness to me and for telling his story with such humour, clarity and honesty.

about the author

C. S. Walton was born in London. She has worked in a variety of jobs, travelled widely and lived in several countries, including Russia. She currently lives in north London.

Also by C.S. Walton: *Little Tenement on the Volga*.